Consuelo Kanaga

An American Photographer

Consuelo Kanaga

An American Photographer

Barbara Head Millstein

Sarah M. Lowe

THE BROOKLYN MUSEUM

in association with

UNIVERSITY OF WASHINGTON PRESS

The publication was organized at
The Brooklyn Museum by Elaine Koss, Editor-in-Chief
Editor: Joanna Ekman
Designer: Dana Levy, Perpetua Press, Los Angeles
Duotone films produced by Eastern Press, New Haven
Printed and bound by South China Printing Co., Hong Kong

The Brooklyn Museum
200 Eastern Parkway
Brooklyn, New York 11238

University of Washington Press
4045 Brooklyn Ave.
Seattle, Washington 98105

The publication of this catalogue was made possible, in part, by
the National Endowment for the Arts, a federal agency; the
Milton and Sally Avery Arts Foundation; Florence D. Lewisohn;
Lucille and Charles M. Plotz; and Kirk and Carolyn Wilkinson.

Library of Congress Cataloging-in-Publication Data
Lowe, Sarah M.
    Consuelo Kanaga : An American photographer / Sarah M.
Lowe, Barbara Head Millstein.
        p.   cm.
    published on the occasion of the exhibition Consuelo
Kanaga, an American photographer, the Brooklyn Museum.
    Includes bibliographical references and index.
    ISBN 0-295-97228-9
    1. Photography, Artistic—Exhibitions. 2. Kanaga,
Consuelo. 1894 —Exhibitions. I. Millstein, Barbara Head.
II. Brooklyn Museum. III. Title.
    TR647.K32   1992
    779'.092—dc20   91-35933
                                           CIP

The paper used in this publication meets the minimum requirements of American National Standard for Information Science—
Permanence of Paper for Printed Materials, ANSI Z39.48-1984.

COVER
Young Girl in Profile, 1948 (Plate 29)

BACK COVER
Creatures on a Rooftop, 1937 (Plate 105)

PAGE 2
Camellia in Water, 1927/28 (Plate 95)

Manufactured in Hong Kong

CONTENTS

FOREWORD

W E AT THE BROOKLYN MUSEUM take pride in
presenting this exhibition celebrating the life
and work of one of America's finest and most
original photographers. *Consuelo Kanaga: An
American Photographer* not only includes the
artist's best-known images such as *She Is a Tree of Life to Them* and *Frances
with Flower* but also introduces the Museum's audience to many of her
photographs never before seen or published. Kanaga's sixty-year career is
highlighted by the 120 photographs in the show; these plus an additional 60
figures by the photographer are illustrated in the catalogue.

It is especially appropriate that The Brooklyn Museum has organized
this tribute to the artist. The Museum's longtime commitment to photography dates back to 1889, when its parent institution, The Brooklyn Institute
of Arts and Sciences, formed a separate department of photography, with an
interest in exhibitions and teaching; the department's first chief instructor was
Clarence White. In 1891 the Museum organized its first photography annual
exhibition, which became a fifty-two-year tradition. Over the years we
presented important exhibitions of artists including Alvin Langdon Coburn,
Arnold Genthe, Gertrude Käsebier, Dorothea Lange, Walker Evans, Ben
Shahn, Joel-Peter Witkin, Charles Sheeler, and Edward Weston, as well as the
first major retrospective of Lewis Wickes Hine, with such distinguished
judges as Alfred Stieglitz and Edward Steichen. In 1976 the department
organized a retrospective of fifty prints by Consuelo Kanaga that resulted in
a major gift of all the photographer's negatives and a substantial number of
prints. This bequest led to the present reconsideration of Kanaga's work.

The scope of the exhibition and breadth of the catalogue are a tribute
to the persistence and dedication of the co-curators, Barbara Head Millstein,
Associate Curator of Painting and Sculpture at The Brooklyn Museum, and
Sarah M. Lowe, guest curator. Their collaboration reflects years of research
and brings together for the first time an extensive presentation of Kanaga's
work. The catalogue summarizes Kanaga's contribution to the history of
photography and details her rich career, revealing much new information on

a subject for which there has been a paucity of published material. We hope that this presentation of Kanaga's oeuvre in the context of twentieth-century American photography will inaugurate new studies of this heretofore neglected major artist.

We would like to take this opportunity to thank William Maxwell for his graceful and informative introduction to the catalogue and for his support thoughout the exhibition. We are also most grateful to Grace M. Mayer for her insight and her postscript to the catalogue, a recollection of Kanaga as Steichen knew her.

Fortunately, we have received generous support from both private and public sources. We gratefully acknowledge the support of the National Endowment for the Arts; the Milton and Sally Avery Arts Foundation; Florence D. Lewisohn; Lucille and Charles M. Plotz; and Kirk and Carolyn Wilkinson.

We also wish to thank the many lenders to the exhibition. Their invaluable contribution has significantly enhanced our presentation of *Consuelo Kanaga: An American Photographer.*

ROBERT T. BUCK
Director

PREFACE
AND
ACKNOWLEDGMENTS

WOMEN HAVE PLAYED A MAJOR ROLE in the history of American Modernist photography, and among the significant players—Berenice Abbott, Imogen Cunningham, Dorothea Lange, Louise Dahl-Wolfe, Marjorie Content, and Tina Modotti—stands Consuelo Kanaga, a friend and admired colleague of these women. Sadly, Kanaga must be counted among the many women photographers who went unrecognized until the end of their careers or who were rediscovered after death, although she was respected by Alfred Stieglitz, Edward Steichen, and Edward Weston, and was instrumental in furthering the careers of Weston, Cunningham, Lange, Dahl-Wolfe, Content, and Modotti, among others. Her impact on many of her peers could only be touched upon in this catalogue, and the full extent of her influence during her lifetime on other photographers is a subject that merits further research.

Truly a bicoastal artist, Kanaga was associated with two photographic landmarks of the first half of the century: on the West Coast, the pivotal *f.64* exhibition of 1932 held in San Francisco; and in the east, the Photo League of New York of the late 1930s and 1940s. Perhaps her activity on both coasts contributed to her lack of public recognition or acceptance in photographic history, although it also extended her illustrious circle of friends, colleagues, and admirers. Nevertheless, until now only her peers and mentors recognized the remarkable power of her photographs. With this exhibition and catalogue, the full range of her talent can begin to be appreciated.

The evidence we have brought together to present this biography of Kanaga and analysis of her contribution to the history of photography is based on four years of research. Because of Kanaga's natural reticence, persistent modesty, and fierce pride, coupled with a careless memory for dates, our pursuit of facts has proved extremely difficult. Kanaga, although a gifted raconteur, revealed few solid facts about her compelling and adventurous life. This biography, we trust, will come as a revelation to some who thought they knew her well. It discloses a woman whose varied experiences during the first half of her career were equal to those generally more available to men: after an early career as a newspaper journalist in the first quarter of the century, followed by a tour of Europe and a stay in an expatriate art colony in North Africa during the 1920s, she became a published photojournalist (in radical periodicals and women's magazines) in the 1930s and a pioneer in photographic abstraction in the 1940s.

Building on the foundation of The Brooklyn Museum's extensive holdings, the curators of this exhibition have endeavored to present Kanaga's varied but consistently matchless photographs to the public and scholarly communities. Kanaga's estate—the bulk of her negatives and nearly 400 prints—was left to the Museum by the late Wallace B. Putnam, Kanaga's last husband. This bequest came as a result of a fifty-print retrospective presented at the Museum through Richard Lerner and the Lerner-Heller Gallery in December 1976.

We extend our gratitude to the many people who have contributed to this project and have made this exhibition and catalogue possible:

Special thanks are due to Kristina Amadeus, whose enthusiasm, research, and all-out cooperation were indispensable for the success of this project.

Kanaga's brother, Amos R. Kanaga, Jr., and her nephew, Marvin (Chick) Brown, have been extremely generous, answering questions and providing details. The late Wallace Putnam was a most helpful source of information about his wife.

Special mention and appreciation go to several people whose previous research on Kanaga expedited our work: Cornelia Cotton, Judith Kalina, Margaretta Mitchell, Lawrence Saphire, and Anne Tucker. They all gave unstintingly of their time and shared interviews, transcripts, correspondence, and other material on Kanaga.

We are indebted to Kanaga's many friends whose memories and insights about her were vital to this project. We thank March Avery, Sally Avery, Zelda Benjamin, Frieda Birnbaum, Philip Cavanaugh, Susan Copen-Oken, Edward Davis, Macdonald Deming, Mansfield and Ruth Esherick, Nicholas and Peggy Freyberg, Helen Gee, Hella Hamid, Mrs. John R. Harrison, Katherine Kuh, Barbara Kulicke, Evelyn Jones, Florence Lewisohn, Jack Manning, William Maxwell, Helen Meredith, Harvey S. S. Miller and J. Randall Plummer, Betty Nelson, Lucille Plotz, Richard Pousette-Dart, Susan Sandberg, Lee Bennett Schreiber, Aaron Siskind, Winn and Lawrence Beal Smith, Rose and Lawrence Treat, Marie Waldron, Kirk and Carolyn Wilkinson.

Maynard Dixon, Hansel Mieth, Ron Partridge, and Peter Stackpole graciously answered questions about the distant past.

Additional invaluable information was provided by Alexander Alland, Jr., Susan Blatchford, Peter Bunnell, Peter Carroll, Susan Ehrens, Mary Ann Flack, Tom Hammang, Christopher Kanaga, Louise LeQuire, Richard Lorenz, Rosemary McNamara, Charles Meyer, Naomi Rosenblum, Jean S. Tucker, and David Vestal.

We would like to thank Helen Coule Lurie for permitting us to read passages from her unpublished autobiography.

We extend our appreciation to the many people who responded to

Fig. 2. Hella Hamid
Consuelo Kanaga and Imogen Cunningham
6¹/₂ x 9¹/₂
X1008.1

Fig. 1. *Berenice Abbott,* 1937
5⁵/₈ x 6¹/₂
Amon Carter Museum,
Fort Worth, Texas

our author's query in *The New York Times Book Review*. Stevie Holland of Culver Pictures deserves a special mention for her persistent research leading to the recovery of thirty-five glass-plate and nitrate negatives by Kanaga.

Numerous curators, librarians, archivists, and museum and gallery personnel have answered scores of inquiries and provided copies of important documents and articles. We would like to express our deep appreciation to the following: Amy Rule, Archivist, and Leslie Calmes, Assistant Archivist, Center for Creative Photography, University of Arizona, Tucson; Martin Antonetti, Special Collections Librarian, Mills College Library, Oakland, California; Sandra Phillips, Curator, Department of Photography, San Francisco Museum of Modern Art; Judith Ames, Research Librarian, Japan Society, New York; Kathleen Correia Euston, Librarian, California Section, California State Library, Sacramento; Suzanne Danos, Public Service Assistant, Beinecke Rare Book and Manuscript Library, Yale University; Librarians Mary Beth Garriott and Judy Nystrom, Grace Doherty Library, Centre College of Kentucky, Danville; Erin Bonner, Librarian and Archivist, The Temporary Contemporary, Los Angeles; Carol Walker Aten, Curatorial Assistant, Addison Gallery of American Art, Phillips Academy, Andover, Massachusetts; David Wooters, Photo Collection, International Museum of Photography at George Eastman House, Rochester, New York; Ann Spalding, Education Coordinator, Maitland Art Center, Maitland, Florida; Barbara C. Polowy, Art and Photography Librarian, Wallace Memorial Library, Rochester Institute of Technology, Rochester, New York; Michael Harvey, Librarian, California Historical Society, San Francisco; Amy Hague, Sophia Smith Collection, Smith College, Northampton, Massachusetts; Anne Matlin, Reference Center for Marxist Studies, Inc., New York; Susan Parker Sherwood, Archivist, Labor Archives and Research Center, San Francisco State University; Kenneth Craven, Archivist, William Randolph Hearst Collection, University of Texas, Austin; Howard Greenberg, Howard Greenberg Gallery, New York; Allen Klotz, Photocollect, New York; Patricia R. Hallinan, John C. Hart Memorial Library, Shrub Oak, New York; Anne and Lou Gordon, Gordon & Gordon Booksellers, West Park, New York.

At The Brooklyn Museum we would like to thank those whose professional expertise and enthusiasm were vital to this project: Robert T. Buck, Roy R. Eddey, Dr. Linda S. Ferber, Elaine Koss, Rena Zurofsky, Larry Clark, Linda Konheim Kramer, Karyn Zieve, Patricia Layman Bazelon, Patty Wallace, Mary Kwiatkowski, Elizabeth Dzuricky de Gonzalez, and Pamela Johnson. Special acknowledgment should go to our editor, Joanna Ekman.

For generous research assistance, Barbara Head Millstein would like to thank Irwin Silver and Leonard Marcus, and for personal encouragement, she thanks Gilbert Millstein.

Sarah M. Lowe would like to thank E. E. Smith for her dependable support and consistently good advice. She respectfully dedicates her work for this catalogue to the Reverend Elmer Miller (1929–1991).

B.H.M. and S.M.L.

NOTE
TO THE
CATALOGUE

Unless otherwise noted in the list of plates (pp. 217–20) or the figure captions, all photographs are in the collection of The Brooklyn Museum: the credit line is Gift of Wallace B. Putnam from the Estate of Consuelo Kanaga. All dimensions are given in inches, and unless otherwise indicated, all photographs are gelatin silver. Modern prints from negatives were printed by Tom Baril and Patty Wallace; accession numbers of the negatives are given for these photographs.

Titles and dates of photographs are given when known. In captions and list of plates, brackets have been used to indicate descriptive titles assigned by the curators. Where there is internal or external evidence to suggest a date, the curators have entered one with "c." Where no date appears, no evidence was available to suggest one.

All plates are reproduced actual size, up to a maximum of $8\,^1/_4$ by $6\,^5/_8$. Plates made through a modern printing of Kanaga's negatives are reproduced the same size as their negatives, with the exception of plates 49, 50, 58, 97, and 98.

The following abbreviations have been used in the notes:

Bender Papers	Albert Bender Papers, Mills College Library, Special Collections, Oakland, California
BHM	Barbara Head Millstein
CK	Consuelo Kanaga
Stieglitz Papers	Stieglitz Collection, Yale Collection of American Literature, Beinecke Rare Book and Manuscript Library, Yale University
SML	Sarah M. Lowe
WPE	Estate of Wallace B. Putnam, Yorktown Heights, New York

INTRODUCTION

William Maxwell

HER VOICE WAS HUSKY and her way of speaking unhurried. And one never knew what strange remark would come out of her mouth. "I dreamt last night I was pursued through the treetops by a gorilla," she said sweetly, with her hand on the teapot. The tea was strong and very good, and with it there would be cookies or a loaf of Indian bread baked that afternoon. On the tea tray was a huge jar of honey, and the mugs we drank from were ironstone, oversized, chipped and discolored with age and use. I sat holding my mug and hoping for a story. Often they were about her growing up in San Francisco. She was her father's child. Her mother didn't understand her and continually fussed at her in an effort to make her more ladylike. This was doomed to failure. She was what she was, the ugly duckling that all artists are when young. Concession was outside her nature. Her stories about her childhood were unsentimental and haunting, and I hung on every word, feeling that this was as close to actual life as it is possible for narrative to get.

The people up and down our country road knew she was a first-rate photographer and were fond of her personally but rather took her for granted, and she did not go in for being important. But once, my wife and I ran into her in a theater lobby in Greenwich Village. She was surrounded by admirers and I realized that here she was a queen.

She spoke gratefully of Edward Steichen. She loved Alfred Stieglitz and detested Georgia O'Keeffe because of the way she treated him. The peace walk in Albany, Georgia, which she took part in, recurred in her conversation and was, I think, one of the high points of her life. Many years after she had focused her camera on them, she continued to love the people she had photographed: a delicate-boned little black girl holding a spray of apple blossoms to her nose; an old woman and a sickly little boy, her grandchild, in a room reeking of poverty and deprivation. And others like them.

She photographed our younger daughter when she was six days old, indoors, where the only light was what came through the windows just after the sun had gone down. The baby's face, with her eyelids covering her eyes, has the smiling inward look of a Cambodian head of Buddha. Somewhat later she photographed our older child sitting on the back steps, barelegged, in a French nursery smock, with a rag doll in her lap and in her two-year-old face the bewilderment and grief of the dispossessed. Connie herself was dispossessed—that is to say, she was in the wrong place. The people she wanted to be photographing were in the city, in black neighborhoods, or in the deep South.

One day she brought us four luster cups that her New England sister-in-law had given her. Family china, and very old, probably valuable, but they didn't—to use a Quaker expression—speak to her condition. And she didn't want them in her house, where there was nothing that was not of its kind rare and in some way like her or her husband, the painter Wallace Putnam. She called him Wal.

A little shining brook flows past the flagstone terrace in front of their house. It was lined on both sides with ferns, crane's bill, black-eyed Susans and wild columbine, and flowers that had gone wild, such as a dark red primrose that was everywhere. She guarded the wild, natural look of the place and grieved over every weed Wally pulled up. She would herself have taken out only enough to bring in a little air. Flowers and weeds were not different to her.

Having in mind her photograph of a gardenia in a glass of water, I took her a white rose from our garden, in a crystal bud vase that my wife had given me for an anniversary present. And in return got a photograph of the underside of a white seagull soaring in the upper atmosphere. Something Connie said to Wally caused him to pick up and throw at her the nearest object, which happened to be my vase with a rose in it. The seagull was by way of amends.

There was only one large exhibition of her work in her lifetime, at Wave Hill in 1977.

She had an affectionate relationship with her nephew, Marvin Brown, who lived with them for a time. Two seventeen-year-old boys of the neighborhood were attracted to her, and she taught them how to use a camera and was worshipped by them.

At the end of her life she remarked to my wife that the cooking utensils of Eskimo women were buried with them. And added, "I know that some woman will turn up to take care of Wal, but I worry about what will happen to my pots and pans, that I have loved so."

Objects survive, and if proper care is taken of them, so do photographs. Survive and are treasured. As I believe the work of Consuelo Kanaga will be. What other photographer perceived the accumulated sorrow in the eye of a cart-horse? Or that a cake of Ivory soap is of the same order of beauty as the frieze on the Parthenon?

CONSUELO KANAGA
An American Photographer

Barbara Head Millstein

The great alchemy is your attitude, who you are, what you are. When you make a photograph, it is very much a picture of your own self. That is the important thing. Most people try to be striking to catch the eye. I think the thing is not to catch the eye but the spirit.

I feel something close to religion in photography.

I thought a medium like photography could change the world.
—CONSUELO KANAGA

CONSUELO KANAGA (1894–1978) is one of America's most transcendent yet, surprisingly, least-known photographers. She disdained wealth and fame throughout her life, and her career, which spanned more than fifty years, has until now remained wrapped in unwarranted obscurity.

Kanaga was indisputably a master printer; she experimented freely in her pursuit of the perfect print. The exquisite tonality she achieved is reproduced mechanically only with great difficulty. But more important, Kanaga's work is so filled with perception, compassion, and honesty that one of her admirers observed, "She gives us her eyes to look at the world."[1]

Her work, although heavily indebted to the Photo-Secession (Stieglitz, Steichen, and Clarence White, among others), was eclectic in its choice of subjects, reflecting an interest at various times in social documentation, near-abstraction, Precisionism, and commercial photography. To this range of images, Kanaga brought consummate technique, humanity, and artistry. Her sensitive and beautiful portraits of African Americans, in particular, are dramatically different from the impersonal and condescending pictures taken by other white photographers of her generation. Her work also reflected her lifelong concern for the poor and disenfranchised.

Consuelo Kanaga was the second child born to Amos Ream Kanaga, Sr. (fig. 4), and Mathilda Carolina Hartwig (fig. 5). A farmer, lawyer, and judge from Bellville, Ohio, Amos Kanaga received his law degree in 1880 from Oberlin College in Ohio. He practiced law locally and then moved to Astoria, Oregon, where he became a successful district attorney. Before 1900 he

Fig. 3. Alma Lavenson
Consuelo Kanaga, c. 1930
Modern print from negative
Courtesy Alma Lavenson Associates
and Susan Ehrens

Left
Fig. 4. *Amos Ream Kanaga, Sr.*
3⁷/₈ x 3
82.65.156

Center
Fig. 5. Consuelo Kanaga (?)
Tillie Kanaga
3¹⁵/₁₆ x 3
Estate of Wallace B. Putnam

Right
Fig. 6. *S. Neva Kanaga Brown*
Modern print from negative
82.65.852

moved with his family to the San Francisco area. According to the Kanaga genealogy, he was an excellent criminal lawyer.[2] A Christian Scientist who maintained high standards for himself and his family, he was a rugged individualist who eventually gave up his law practice to publish agricultural journals. Preoccupied with agronomy and fond of travel, he would pick up at a moment's notice with or without his wife and children, often leaving them to fend for themselves.[3]

Like her husband, "Tillie" Kanaga had a strong personality, indomitable and independent. She compiled the popular and still useful *History of Napa Vally* (1901) and later became a real estate broker, then an unusual occupation for a woman.

The oldest child was Sarah Neva (called Neva) (fig. 6), born in 1891. Consuelo Delesseps (called Connie) followed in 1894. Another daughter, Yvette, died at the age of eleven, but the date of her birth is now impossible to ascertain. The youngest—Amos, Jr. (fig. 7)—was born fourteen years after Consuelo, in 1908. Neva became an artist who wrote and illustrated children's books. Amos junior started his career early as an amateur puppeteer and later became a professional ventriloquist, traveling the vaudeville circuits. A gifted inventor, he finally settled down and began his own successful manufacturing business.

Family lore has it that Kanaga's mother so admired Ferdinand-Marie de Lesseps, the builder associated with the Suez and Panama canals, that she wrote to him asking if she could name her daughter Consuelo de Lesseps after his wife. Since neither of his two wives was named Consuelo and he died in 1894, the year of Connie's birth, the story appears to be apocryphal. Family mythology also suggests that the name Kanaga was a form of Carnegie and that it was changed because of some family financial scandal.[4] According to the family genealogy, however, the name is Swiss and dates back at least 250 years.

Amos senior thought it was vital that his children get to know the

Fig. 7. Attributed to Consuelo Kanaga
Consuelo Kanaga and Amos Kanaga, Jr., c. 1915
Courtesy Amos Kanaga, Jr.

world and do some traveling. As Kanaga said: "Our father felt travel more important than schooling." Some of his business trips with Connie and Neva took them to the Mexican border, where the local Indians made a great impression on Connie. Of their travels throughout the West, she wrote: "It was exciting—we rode in stagecoaches, played with Indian children, stayed in hotels with burlap walls (bath $5, glass of water 50 cents), cowboys everywhere." When she was only eight or nine, she was told about an Indian boy who kept running away from "the white man's" school. She spoke of this incident as her first social awareness and often related a story revealing an early concern for people in prison. When Kanaga was about thirteen and her family lived near Sausalito, she paddled a kayak out near Alcatraz. She took along a sandwich and a rope, prepared to help any prisoner who might be swimming to freedom.[5]

When Tillie "showed signs of fatigue," Kanaga recalled that "Papa decided we should know the joys of farm life as he had known them on his father's farm in Ohio. We boarded at large dairy farms, played with the farmer's children in the hayloft, went to a one-room schoolhouse, spelling bees, Saturday night baths in a big round tub in the kitchen. Mother far from resting, disappeared for weeks at a time in her horse and buggy gathering data for a now prized History of Napa County."

Kanaga adored her mother and vied with Neva for her attention. She fought often with her older sister, who intimidated her and whom she considered far more clever than herself.[6] Tillie tried to instill standards of mannerly behavior in all of her children with little success, failing particularly to make Consuelo behave in a ladylike way. She considered Connie too much of a tomboy to be taken to restaurants or hotels with the rest of the family; finding Neva's behavior more conventional, she took her everywhere. According to a friend of Connie's, Tillie was a "bubble buster"; Connie loved

Fig. 8. Photographer unknown
Consuelo Kanaga (San Francisco), c. late 1910s
7⅞ x 6⅛
Estate of Wallace B. Putnam

mischief, was strong-minded and opinionated, and got her "romantic quality" from her mother.[7]

Kanaga's memories of her childhood convey a sense of loneliness. Devoted to her father and miserable when he was away on his many trips, Connie spent a great deal of time by herself. Since the Kanagas boarded in rooming houses and farms while Amos senior was away on his business trips, she made few friends outside of the family. She consoled herself by reading omnivorously and by treasuring her few childhood secrets, and she enjoyed being more than a little mysterious for the rest of her life. Her solitary existence taught her independence. She was never afraid to be alone or to travel alone for most of her adult life.

Both of Kanaga's parents were writers, and her father encouraged her to write, which she did well. As a young woman, she kept a dream diary for several years.[8] She was a poor student, however. She often related a story about dreading an important spelling test at the age of twelve and wishing fervently for divine intervention. It was 1906, the eve of the great San Francisco fire and earthquake. Convinced that she was at least partly responsible for the catastrophe, she determined to end her formal education with high school.[9] Kanaga was a consummate storyteller who enchanted her friends with this talent throughout her life.

No sources reveal what Kanaga did between graduating from high school and working professionally. One can only speculate that she might have worked under her father's supervision for his publications, *Farm and Irrigation Age* and *Machinery Trade Journal*, before seeking her personal independence in 1915 at the age of twenty-one, applying for a job on *The San Francisco Chronicle*. Hired as a reporter and feature writer, a rare profession for a woman in those days, she soon discovered that her articles required photographs and accompanied the photographer to suggest ways to make the pictures more interesting. The editor liked the results and urged her to learn photography.

She was apparently good at supervising the photo setups, and with the editor's support and a promise of a big raise (which did not particularly interest her), she eagerly went into the darkroom to learn the business, as she said, "from a to z." Despite the arduous job of carrying the large, heavy camera used in those days and the lack of encouragement from her father, "who was outraged at my being anything as low as a photographer,"[10] Kanaga found the work interesting and was eager to learn. She began her apprenticeship by filing thousands of glass negatives and mixing chemicals, gallons at a time. She lived in the darkroom, breathing noxious fumes and "sweating blood" to get the results she wanted. Here she learned her craft. She remembered: "We had a full tank of film but we could examine [the plates] one at a time. If they were developing too fast, we could put them in water or finish them. We could watch every step because they were in open tanks and we could use a chemical called pinacryptol green which would permit you to examine the film by a fair darkroom light."[11] It was a big newspaper and she was serving all the photographers. She made copy prints and copy negatives. After she had learned printing, enlarging, and developing, she became a newspaper photographer, covering every kind of story from society news to striking lettuce pickers.

Left
Fig. 9. *Portrait of a Woman*
$3^3/_4 \times 2^5/_8$
82.65.214

Right
Fig. 10. *Portrait of a Woman*
Gelatin silver toned print
$2^3/_8 \times 2^1/_4$
82.65.303

Once she had mastered newspaper photography, it began to interest her less. She joined the California Camera Club, where she met other photographers. The Camera Club was small and had a darkroom that Kanaga could use as she wished. It was at the club that she first saw Alfred Stieglitz's *Camera Work.* "It changed my life," she said. She felt that the prints were "the most beautiful things that had ever been done in photography, and I wanted to start from there."[12]

It was also at the California Camera Club that she met Dorothea Lange, who became a friend. In 1961 Lange remembered Kanaga as the first female newspaper photographer she had ever encountered: "She was a person way ahead of her time, Consuelo. She was a terribly attractive, dashing kind of gal, who . . . lived in a Portuguese hotel in North Beach, which was entirely Portuguese working men, except Consuelo. She's . . . a sweet, simple person. But she had more courage! She'd go anywhere and do anything. She was perfectly able, physically, to do anything at anytime the paper told her to. They could send her to places where an unattached woman shouldn't be sent and Consuelo was never scathed. . . . She was a dasher. . . . She was very— generally if you use the word unconventional you mean someone who breaks the rules—she had no rules. Never has had."[13]

Cutting her newspaper work down to two or three days a week and working as a stringer, or free-lance newspaper worker, Kanaga also did private portraiture. Through one of her clients, Mrs. John R. Harrison, then president of the Junior League in San Francisco, Kanaga was introduced to the lucrative work of society photography. She found portraiture the most fulfilling work, and although she preferred to photograph striking grape

Fig. 11. Consuelo Kanaga (?)
Louise Dahl (San Francisco), c. 1910s
Gelatin silver toned print
4⅝ x 6¹⁵/₁₆
Estate of Wallace B. Putnam, Courtesy of
Kristina Amadeus

pickers, she didn't mind doing portraits of brides and grandchildren, subjects she could choose as she wished.[14] According to Mrs. Harrison, Kanaga was offered a job on the *San Francisco Examiner* by Mrs. William Randolph Hearst, but she refused it because of her disapproval of Hearst's politics.

A perfectionist, Kanaga put her entire effort into her work, making as many as fifty prints before she would find one that suited her. This obsession with perfection in printing became a theme of her artistic life and was the reason her production was so limited. As she said many years later, "That's why I never did get rich."[15]

In 1919, when Kanaga was twenty-five, she switched employers briefly, moving to the *San Francisco Daily News*. About that time she married a childhood sweetheart, Evans Davidson, a mining engineer.[16] According to those who remembered him, he was a gentle man, and the couple appeared to be very much in love. One of the problems with the marriage was that Kanaga preferred city life. It was there that she felt most stimulated by her subjects; she wanted to photograph people. Although she loved Davidson, he refused to live in a city. Moreover, his job kept them separated for months at a time. The marriage lasted only about two or three years.[17]

In 1920 Kanaga moved with her family to 4228 Twenty-sixth Street and eventually established a separate studio.[18] Kanaga said of herself in retrospect: "I never made a big living, but a small living and lots of joy. Lots of caring and feeling went into the making of my pictures. At that time I was doing mainly portraits. I had to learn to do something so that I could at least make a living. My family wasn't well to do. They weren't poor but they could not keep me in the state of photographic bliss I wanted. I wouldn't have taken their money if they had it. I was very independent."[19]

Kanaga continued to share her time between newspaper work and society portraiture, with time out for an occasional project of her own. To satisfy her "creative" side, she saved two days out of every week to look for "something beautiful" and then shoot it, develop it, and print for her own gratification.[20]

With her friend Louise Dahl (fig. 11), whom she taught to use a $3^{1}/_{4}$-by-$4^{1}/_{4}$ camera with a soft-focus lens, she would roam the city on Sundays, looking for exciting subjects to photograph, mostly around Chinatown or Russian Hill. They very much admired the work of Arnold Genthe and Francis Bruguière.[21]

Kanaga's circle of friends may well have included Imogen Cunningham, Ansel Adams, and Edward Weston (with whom she later showed in the Group f.64 exhibition of 1932), and perhaps the Italian-born actress (soon to be photographer) Tina Modotti. Her friends respected her work as a journalist and often asked her advice. Sometimes she found them jobs. Most important in terms of her blossoming career was her friendship with the art patron Albert Bender, who encouraged her to widen her intellectual frame of reference and also helped her to find more profitable commissions.

Sometime in 1922 Kanaga, eager to see more of the United States and with the intention of ending her journey in New York City, drove east (before there were interstate highways) with a couple she had just met, ending up in Denver with no money. The story she told is that after she quickly landed a job as a newspaper photographer, she was sent to cover a rodeo, where two bashful cowboys took an interest in her and staked her to money for the rest of her trip by rail and steamer. She had been living on beans.[22]

It is possible that before heading for New York, Kanaga made her way to New Orleans, where she met a woman named May (fig. 12). They found a place to live in the French Quarter, where Kanaga set up a rudimentary photo studio to make enough money to get her to New York. The two women traveled freely around the city and into the countryside. The large tripod and camera Kanaga always carried made them look respectable and warded off unpleasant encounters. Kanaga photographed a nearby farm and some children in the French Quarter. After a couple of months, she had earned enough money to continue her journey.[23]

Soon after arriving in New York Harbor at 6:00 A.M. on September 18, 1922,[24] Kanaga took a job on William Randolph Hearst's *New York American*, a morning newspaper, very likely as a features photographer, despite her earlier scruples. During the following year, she worked intermittently, only photographing for one of Mrs. Hearst's favorite charities, the New York American Christmas and Relief Fund, established by Hearst in 1908.[25] Kanaga's photographs were to be used during the month of December on a page called "News of the Day in Pictures," which always included a charity shot or two, with a roundup on December 24 and 25. She shot only three or four photographs, using a Graflex, and it took her about six months (plates 5–7). As she said, "I had plenty of time to look around."[26]

But most important, soon after her arrival in New York, she met Alfred Stieglitz, the man who had changed her life and her mind about photography through his publication *Camera Work*: "The cuts [in *Camera*

Fig. 12. *May [Spear?]*, c. early 1920s
Gelatin silver toned print
4 x 3
82.65.328

Work] were so beautiful and different from anything that I had seen, and I just thought that this was *it*." She recalled meeting Stieglitz: "A friend took me to call on him and then I saw him from time to time in his gallery. I didn't have a portfolio in those days, so I took one or two prints in to show him. I never had enough to show [him], I was so busy trying to make a few good photographs that I could look at."[27]

Shortly after Kanaga had gone to work for the Hearst publication, she met and apparently fell in love with an aspiring young artist, Donald Litchfield, an Englishman several years younger than herself who worked as a retoucher and layout man at *The New York American*.[28] By March they were sharing an apartment at 17 Christopher Street in Greenwich Village.[29] It was most certainly Litchfield who persuaded Stieglitz to look at Kanaga's photographs. He sent Stieglitz a print of *Fire* in winter 1922 by way of introduction to her work.[30] Litchfield had been acquainted with Stieglitz for some time; they had carried on a philosophical correspondence since at least 1917. Stieglitz encouraged the friendship of talented and intelligent young artists, and Litchfield, highly opinionated and a womanizer (according to his correspondence),[31] confided both his artistic ideas and his most intimate thoughts on life, sex, and love to the older photographer, referring to him on occasion as "the all knowing one."[32] It is unclear how their friendship actually began.

Kanaga herself began a formal friendship with Stieglitz. On January 13, 1923, she wrote to him from her apartment at 109 Bedford Street in Greenwich Village[33] to thank him for showing her his work the previous Saturday. "It has meant a great deal to me," she wrote, and then added: "I thought photography had limitations. Now realizing they are within myself I can go on." In a letter of June 6, she told him that she had seen Paul Rosenfeld's book, *Port of New York*, and enjoyed Stieglitz's photographs in it, "particularly the one of Miss O'Keeffe, immensely." In an undated letter from San Francisco inscribed "Christmas Morning," she wrote with feeling of the impact Stieglitz's work had had on her:

> For years now I have carried about with me the image of your photographs.
>
> No gift has come so near me nor no possession so dear as having seen and known your work.
>
> It is not your technique alone but more some ringing message of truth and fearlessness which has helped me in living."[34]

Kanaga and Litchfield tried to eke out a living in New York City, but in early July 1924 they departed by train for the West Coast.[35] Soon after their arrival in California, they stayed for a short while at a country place belonging to Kanaga's sister, Neva, in Capitola, near Santa Cruz.[36] Circumstances then forced them to live apart for several months; Kanaga moved back to San Francisco to seek a divorce from Davidson, to work on her career, and to make some money from doing portraits, while Litchfield accepted a good job offer with a newspaper in Los Angeles.[37] After he was fired in February 1925, he joined Kanaga in San Francisco,[38] but they were forced to live separately for a year to fulfill the requirements for her divorce.[39] In August Litchfield began an affair with a younger woman that effectively ended the relationship with

Kanaga, which had been intermittently strained over the past year.[40] In later correspondence with Stieglitz, he regretted his behavior, concluding in 1929: "Sometimes I think of Consuelo—she really was OK & with my present experience I believe I or we could have made a go—she was the 'straightest' woman I ever knew."[41]

By September Kanaga had established a studio at 1371 Post Street near her good friend Albert Bender. A patron of literature, painting, sculpture, music, and dance, Bender fully understood the significance of photography as an art form. He attracted a wide circle of talented people who revered him. Among the photographers he chose to encourage were Imogen Cunningham, Alma Lavenson, Louise Dahl, Edward Weston, Ansel Adams, and Consuelo Kanaga.[42]

In Kanaga's case he not only found her commissions but, on occasion, managed her finances, an area she found confusing and distracting. Along with Alfred Stieglitz, he widened her frame of reference with respect to literature, music, and art, and he urged her to take a couple of years to travel and photograph in Europe.

In late March 1927, Kanaga at the age of thirty-two set off for Europe on a journey of self-discovery.

Before going east, en route to Europe, Kanaga stopped to see her good friend Edward Weston. She admired Weston's photographs, though she could not help teasing him about the speed with which he printed (ten negatives in two hours); he brooded over a gibe she once tossed at him about a famous New York photographer who made one "perfect" negative a year.[43] Nevertheless, she tried to help his career. Weston hoped "to try for an exhibit the next season," and as Kanaga left for New York, she took along a number of his prints to drop off with Alfred Stieglitz.[44] (Stieglitz eventually rejected the prints. As Kanaga wrote Weston in May, "He thought your technique was very fine but felt the prints lacked life, fire, were more or less dead things not a part of today."[45]) When Kanaga left New York about March 20, she warned Weston of the drawbacks of becoming part of Stieglitz's circle: "[He] will keep you in your place, you will always be known as one of the Stieglitz group, and his power in New York is tremendous."[46]

An extraordinary series of more than fifty letters between Kanaga and Bender (primarily from Kanaga) written during this period not only provides details of her trip abroad, but also charts her intellectual and artistic growth. The correspondence also makes us privy to the delicate balance of control that inevitably characterizes the artist-patron relationship. Kanaga had made arrangements for Bender to handle her $2,000 for the trip. Bender sent the first check for $500 to Thomas Cook & Sons in Paris, suggesting that on her return to the United States she have at least $1,000 "to start the world anew."[47]

Arriving in Paris on June 8, 1927,[48] Kanaga stayed in the city only a short while, leaving after only a few weeks for Concarneau, an artists' colony on the coast of Brittany. She planned to meet her friends Louise Dahl and Anna Cohn some months later in Paris and to continue traveling with Dahl.

Kanaga may have decided to retreat to Concarneau when she received word soon after her arrival in Paris that her father had died in April. Before she had left San Francisco, he had begged her not to go abroad, pleading that he might never see her again. She had nevertheless determined to make the journey, but this decision may have caused her some guilt. In later years she often repeated the story that soon after his death her father appeared to her in a dream surrounded by glittering glass, telling her that he was thankful that death was something to be desired.[49]

In Concarneau she stayed in a tiny attic in a pension, and her correspondence with Bender indicates that her sojourn there was a time of reflection. She seems to have been able to confide in Bender, whom she told: "Your understanding and friendship are precious to have. It means more to me that you know something of my inner life and workings than that I am just one of your very many friends."[50] It is unlikely that they shared an intimate relationship, and perhaps for this reason she felt free to reveal herself without fear of being hurt. She told Bender, "Life can be very lovely but I find it most beautiful away from human beings." She took her greatest comfort from nature and expressed disappointment with people, especially men. Later she became even more disillusioned and wrote of her disgust for art colonies and the parasites they attract.[51]

In Concarneau, where she would stay through August, she took up watercolors because she had no adequate camera equipment, promising herself that she would buy proper lenses and even a fine camera when she reached Germany. She had only a soft-portrait lens at the time. Bender advised her to abandon her experiments with watercolor, but she replied that she had been without camera equipment for nearly four months and that her desire for artistic self-expression had to be served. She wrote: "Watercolors are a great joy, very free and spontaneous. The watercolors delight me and playing freely with color is like escaping from the rigorous discipline of photography."[52] She continued to work in watercolor and pastel until the end of her life.

Her correspondence with Bender confirms her early and consistent sympathy and admiration for people of color. Suggesting the possibility of sharing a studio in Paris with a Japanese friend from San Francisco, Eiko Yamazawa (plate 42), whom she had taught photography (and who later became a successful photographer in Japan), she said she would like "Ei" to have a "taste of France because here there are no color distinctions whatsoever." She explained: "The most beautiful white women are freely seen with Negroes. I believe it is wonderful. I am sick of seeing colored men and women abused by stupid white people. How terrible to be a Negro, to have no place, as the American Negro for instance." She told Bender: "In Paris one day I saw the first Negro. . . . He was tall and beautiful and proud and there was none of the insolence, the aggressiveness of our Negroes in America. He was like a child who knows it is welcome and loved and I must admit to see his fine tranquil face was a great joy to me. The first free Negro I had ever seen."[53] Although naïve by today's standards, her response was enlightened for its time.

During the last few weeks in July, Kanaga's personal and philosophical observations to Bender became more revealing, and none are so poignant or acute as those in a letter written sometime between July 22 and August 28. In reply to some encouraging observation of Bender's, she wrote: "I don't feel this wonderful youth you speak of dearest Albert. I am quite seasoned and a little sad and still lonely inside of me. As Gauguin writes, 'I want to love and I cannot—I want not to love and I cannot.'" She confided a longing to have a child: "In Paris I was sick with the desire for a child. I have often felt it be- fore. . . . I felt that strange experience within me that only a childless woman can know—a death of the unborn. . . . To marry for a child seems so dishonest unless there is a true love element in the marriage. I often think of the [many] difficulties of having a child out of wedlock. . . . However it is worthy of consideration."[54]

In her letters from Concarneau, she mentioned reading Eastern popular philosophy in her search for self-knowledge, referring to *The Dance of Siva*, by Ananda Coomaraswamy. She also dipped into Nietzsche, conclud- ing from both that "we are not saved by what we do, only by what we are."[55] Hoping to find enrichment as a photographer rather than success, she sought answers and found comfort in both philosophies.

Kanaga returned to Paris in late August, refreshed by her solitude in Concarneau—she wrote Bender that she had been drinking less and con- cluded that she was happy[56]—and ready for the company of Louise Dahl and Anna Cohn. Her experiences abroad led her to reflect on her feelings about being an American. Struck by the way Americans were treated in France, she sympathized with the Frenchman's horror of American incivility but de- fended the "force and vigor" of Americans, telling Bender, "I wouldn't want to be from any other country."[57]

Kanaga was acquiring a growing sophistication about the work of contemporary artists and more assurance about her own opinions: "Just had a most interesting conversation with Mahonri Young, one of the best American sculptors in Paris. He is real and sincere and had some interesting observations on photography."[58] In October she wrote Bender: "In a way I am sorry you are arranging another Diego [Rivera] Exhibition. He has become so well shown lately and there is a young Mexican artist of great and subtle talent who is practically unknown in California. Edward Weston who has photo- graphed much of his work along with others feels he is [as] worthy of being known and appreciated as Rivera. His name is Jean Charlot."[59]

On October 2 Kanaga set off alone for Germany, intending to meet Dahl and Cohn in Vienna, traveling first to Heidelberg, Würzburg, Rothen- burg, Nuremberg (where she bought a little camera), and Munich.

Her letters from Europe indicate that she was excited by contempo- rary German (and later, Austrian) photography, though perhaps over- whelmed by the avant-garde photomontage and collage that was displacing Pictorialism. At the time she would have seen the Bauhaus photographers Kurt Schwitters, Raoul Hausmann, Lucia Moholy, and László Moholy-Nagy, as well as the Dadaists. She mused: "They do many effective but artificial things here in Germany and I want to know how it all is done without maybe using it as I prefer the purer technique."[60] She despaired of finding photog- raphy with which she could identify: "It seems impossible to meet or talk with photographers as no one speaks English and I speak no German. Besides it is so difficult to know where the best of things are to be found."[61]

In contrast, she was confident in her critical response to a book of

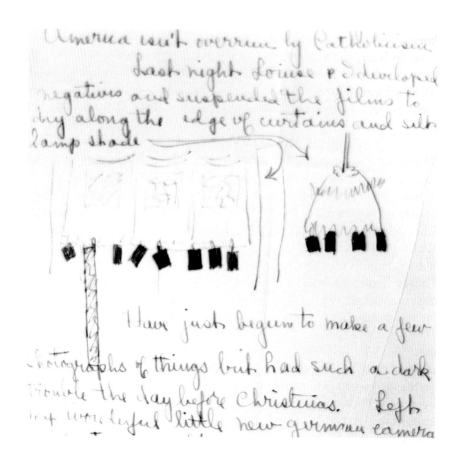

photographs of America by Emile Otto Hoppe (1878–1972), a German photographer who had moved to London in 1907: "[He] has rather a nerve to make a book of a country he has so little understanding of, his work so lacks in feeling." Her annoyance with his pictures of San Francisco, in particular, galvanized her to vow to do her own book of photographs of the West and San Francisco.[62]

Arriving in Vienna on October 27, Kanaga was depressed by the number of beggars she saw in the streets, observing, "Poverty is everywhere."[63] There she met a young Pole who taught modern poster design at "the Peoples School" (probably the Wiener Werkstätte) and arranged a three-day visit: "It is the most fascinating school with sculpture, appreciation of abstract design, tapestry, pottery and fine printing. There is no teaching only guiding and the beauty sense is allowed free scope. It alone was worth a trip to Europe."[64]

Kanaga and Dahl arrived on November 15 in Budapest, where the wife of J. Nilsen Laurvik, the San Francisco museum director and critic and a friend of Bender's, acted as their guide. On November 21 they left Budapest to spend several days in Venice, which Kanaga labeled "an ancient Coney Island kept alive by tourists."[65] While there, however, she produced some of her loveliest European photographs (plates 59–64).

The two women traveled on to Florence, where they stayed for nearly three weeks. By December 4 Kanaga had set up a tiny darkroom in their washroom, hanging a dress over the window to keep out the light, and had bought some supplies. There she eagerly developed the photographs she had taken in Budapest, Venice, and Florence: "It fills me with a fever to have a decent darkroom and equipment and work once more. On the whole I haven't absorbed so much photographically as in a living way."[66] Meanwhile, Dahl, a more serious traveler, was teaching Kanaga to look at architecture and use the guidebooks.

The two photographers spent a week in Rome at Christmastime. They developed more of their negatives, suspending the films to dry along the edges of the curtains and the silk lampshades in their room, sending a sketch of what they had done to Bender (fig. 13).[67] Kanaga had a little too much cognac on Christmas Day and accidentally set fire to the fourteen-inch Christmas tree and Santa Claus that the women had set up in their room. "Louise heaped abuse upon me and I didn't dare say a word because I knew that 14 inches of Merry Xmas meant much to her," she wrote Bender.[68] Kanaga herself, basically an iconoclast, had no use for Catholicism and organized religion in general, though throughout her life, she retained an interest in Eastern religions and the most recondite mystical theology. When Dahl vowed to visit the Pope, Kanaga wrote Bender, "I'm not very curious as most politicians look more or less alike."[69] She found the Sistine Chapel oppressive, remarking that Michelangelo's *Last Judgment* "seemed the puerile, fearful, last clutch at heaven of a frightened old man."[70] Impressed by the Egyptian and Archaic Greek sculpture in Rome, she was offended by the "fig leaves plastered on the purest of conceptions of the Greeks." She was at once indignant and amused at the contradiction between the censored statuary and the earthy behavior of the Italian men.[71]

Despite the beauty of the Italian museums and churches, Dahl and Kanaga, who was down to the last of her money, were anxious to be on their way Palermo and the boat that would take them to Tunisia in North Africa. On January 9, 1928, they set sail for Tunis.

En route, fate and Kanaga's romantic nature combined to change the course of her life radically. From Kairouan, Tunisia, she wrote to Bender: "Coming to Africa on the boat I met a man and it seems we have fallen very much in love with one another."[72] Two weeks after meeting Barry McCarthy, an Irishman and a journalist, she wrote: "To feel the presence and person of another human being entirely is the most wonderful experience I have ever known and Albert dear, this happiness is so beautiful. . . . I can hardly believe it is a part of living for life has seemed a rather flat experience and hardly worth the living really. I have never before known love in which I could bury myself completely." The couple decided to stay in Kairouan for several months: "Just now we will linger here in Africa. . . . I feel the desire to express something of this small tho lovely white city in photography. . . . I want to make a series of photographs which Barry may do an article for."[73]

Kanaga, McCarthy, and Dahl met friends in Kairouan, the artist Harry Shokler, whom Kanaga had known in New York City, and his good friend (later his wife) Dahris Martin, a writer. There Dahl met the man she would eventually marry and work with for most of her life: Meyer (Mike) Wolfe, a painter (fig. 14). She and Kanaga photographed continually in the Tunisian city. Sometime in early March, Kanaga and McCarthy married.[74]

By April 12, 1928, Bender had sent, on Kanaga's request, the balance of her money, the sum of $484.10, which was to have been her nest egg to start life anew in the United States.[75] Penniless, the young couple abandoned designs for a life in Paris and embarked for New York, arriving in early May and soon moving to a furnished room with a gas-plate stove at 9 Charles Street in Greenwich Village.

Despite their lack of funds, Kanaga, with McCarthy's encouragement, turned down a "swell salary offered to me on a Yellow Picture Paper [most likely a Hearst publication], which revolted me so that I wanted to weep at the thought." McCarthy, meanwhile, was hired from "some 2000 applicants to work on a philosophic treatise and spends part of his time writing detective stories." Fortunately, she soon found a job as a retoucher for the commercial studio photographer Nickolas Muray. There, she planned to learn about running a studio properly and, most important, about the art of retouching, which had always intrigued her. She was mystified when she landed the job in the "face of about 18 professional retouchers," still unaware of her own compelling personality and striking appearance.[76] Tension arose between Kanaga and her husband over the job: she left Muray's at McCarthy's insistence several months later. She had resisted her husband's pressure as long as she could because, as she wrote Bender, "I was learning too much and it has just been the past few weeks that made me know I had learned all I could from Mr. Muray." She added: "You see I had never worked on the negative and didn't know much about retouching or etching. I feel quite proud of all I have learned." She had discovered "every angle of how a well run studio should be equipped. . . . There are a thousand efficient devices to save labor and get results I had never suspected."[77]

Around June the couple moved to a converted stable with two rooms and bath at 5 MacDougal Alley. Kanaga's friend Eiko came to visit them that summer, and Kanaga found her temporary work as a retoucher at Muray's studio.

Kanaga by this time felt ready to try to establish herself as a portrait photographer in New York, though she missed San Francisco. In a rare moment of practicality, she admitted to Bender: "I have put in all of my worst years searching and acquiring what knowledge I could and I should be thinking of making money." Her job with Muray had greatly increased her skill but disillusioned her somewhat. Her observation of Muray's business practices led her to believe that reputations were built on the high fee one dared to charge. She suggested that Edward Steichen had gained success in proportion to his inflated fees although "his present work doesn't compare with his earlier work when he was quite poor."[78]

Kanaga may have found it difficult to get work because she had left her portfolio in Kairouan with a young missionary couple who had been called away just before she had to leave for America. The portfolio may never have been returned; in any case, most of Kanaga's work from her European and African trip remains only in the form of two albums or in negative form. Because she rarely felt real confidence in her photographs up until this time, she did not admit to herself that the loss was significant.[79]

While in New York, Kanaga kept Bender informed of her activities and achievements and those of her husband. By summer she had acquired her own enlarging machine, new lights, and new papers and chemicals. She wrote Bender: "I feel again like a beginner and my work looks strange and stiff. Still in time I hope to become more plastic and at ease." She continued, "It seems strange to be trying to accomplish photography here without knowing people but I suppose it is a matter of time and having patience and courage."[80]

Kanaga's letters to Bender may have served a double purpose. She obviously loved and respected him, but she also knew that he had an enduring concern for living artists that superseded his wish to own art. She must have hoped that her patron and friend would approve of her new husband and eventually draw McCarthy into his circle of talented friends who benefited from his support. Her correspondence with Bender slowed as she grew more and more apprehensive about her husband's lack of ambition coupled with his tendency to discourage her desire for a career in photography.

An incident of early autumn 1928 raises questions about mounting tension in Kanaga's marriage. After having worked hard retouching some negatives of portraits, she wrote Bender that she found them lying in the street outside her apartment.[81] The mystery of the discarded negatives is open to several explanations. Kanaga may have had too much to drink and thrown them away by mistake. Another possibility is that McCarthy, finding her intense preoccupation with her work difficult to accept, tossed the negatives into the alley.

This incident notwithstanding, Kanaga continued to receive orders for commercial work and to experiment with "secrets [of printing] which make a tremendous difference in even old negatives." She also deepened her interest in portraiture: "Strange but the more I see in portrait work the nearer I feel toward expressing myself. Now I can see how hours passed absorbing the

quality of painting and sculpture abroad has given me a longing for more clear and penetrating work."[82] "I would sacrifice resemblance, any day to get the inner feeling of a person," she later wrote. "It seems so much more of one than our face which is so often just a mask."[83]

At the Christmas season in 1928, Kanaga found herself alone when McCarthy left for a six-week trip to Cannes.[84] She took the opportunity to "venture forth in search of adventure [with her camera] on the East side or Bowery or Broadway or most any place," finding her experiences "always amazing." At this time she had begun to take some of her most interesting photographs, concentrating on the unemployed and needy.[85] Her skill at darkroom work had invested her imagery with increasing power. By 1930 she stated firmly, "I want to photograph as painters paint, with flowers, forms and from a purely aesthetic point of view."[86]

Although Kanaga realized that New York was a place of "almost unlimited opportunity" and acknowledged that "struggle and difficulties seem to sharpen one's edge,"[87] she admitted, "I am not so young or quite so powerful as I thought I was."[88] Financial problems together with Kanaga's desire to return to the West Coast most likely drove the couple to leave for San Francisco in December 1930. There they moved into Tillie Kanaga's house at 4228 Twenty-sixth Street.[89]

On her return to San Francisco, Kanaga resumed her friendship with the photographers she had met through the California Camera Club. She immediately wrote to Weston, praising his recent photographs and telling of her plans to move and have a darkroom he could share for "town sittings."[90] Later that year he spent an evening with Kanaga discussing his relationship with Stieglitz.[91] She saw Dorothea Lange frequently, as well as Imogen Cunningham and the other members of the Camera Club, all of whom admired and respected her work and considered that her pioneering role as a newspaper photographer gave her special panache.

Several of these photographers formed an informal association that broke away from pictorialist photography, calling themselves Group f.64. The photographer Preston Holder arrived at the name "f.64" (the smallest lens opening, or "stop," providing the sharpest resolution and depth of field), although he was not a member. The group, whose original members were Imogen Cunningham, Ansel Adams, John Paul Edwards, Sonya Noskowiak, Henry Swift, Willard Van Dyke, and Edward Weston, met at 683 Brockhurst Avenue in Oakland and in 1932 organized a gallery in the photographer Annie Brigman's former studio, calling it "683" in deference to Stieglitz's "291" Gallery of the Photo-Secession.[92] Kanaga did not seek to become a member, although she did frequent the gallery: she was too busy rebuilding her career on the West Coast. In June 1932 she was included in the first exhibition of photography at the M. H. de Young Memorial Museum, called *Showing of Hands*,[93] and she was invited to show her work at the landmark *f.64* exhibition that opened at the same museum on November 15 under the direction of Lloyd Page Rollins.[94] Ansel Adams suggested that the group include exclusively the seven original members, "who are striving to define photography as an art form by a simple and direct presentation through purely photographic methods,"[95] but the show of eighty prints also included sixteen photographs by four invited photographers: Alma Lavenson, Preston Holder, Brett Weston (son of Edward Weston), and Consuelo Kanaga.

Of the four photographs contributed by Kanaga, two were most likely of Eluard Luchell McDaniel, a young man befriended by the Kanaga family (plate 31), and two were of a woman named Frances who worked for a friend of Kanaga's (plate 30, fig. 16). "I thought she was lovely," Kanaga said of her model, "so we got a flower and we made this photograph, and it had to be sharp to do a flower against a face like that and have it all clean and alive. It had to be stopped down."[96]

Some forty years later, Kanaga recalled the public reaction to the *f.64* exhibition: "There was one art magazine in San Francisco. Someone wrote a review of it, and [he] spoke of my photographs as immutable, and I was terribly impressed by that. I had never been written up before. I was quite a young photographer, and the word immutable was a big word to have said about your work. I remember that Edward [Weston] and I were the only ones praised."[97]

In the same interview, she expressed some criticism of the Group f.64 approach: "I think the tendency began to get more and more towards sharper photographs until it was just dull. Everything had to be so pin sharp and a lot of beauty in photography was lost, the values and tones that went with soft focus Steichens . . . [that] were just glorious." She further suggested that aside from the common sharpness of focus of the works in the show, the photographers of the group differed greatly: "There were hardly two photographers alike."[98]

Kanaga maintained that she had never believed in the philosophy of Group f.64. She knew only four of the original members, as friends: "The truth is I didn't know them all, or if I did, I had just barely met them. Edward [Weston], Imogen [Cunningham], Willard [Van Dyke], and Ansel [Adams] were the ones I knew." She said it never dawned on her to discuss theories of photography with the members. She wasn't concerned about whether the lens was stopped down or not, she asserted; she felt that the picture determined the focus. As a professional photographer, she saw herself as different from most of Group f.64: "Some of the f.64 group didn't even do portraits. They were just photographing. They would do the house, or maybe their family, a door, or just things they wanted to photograph." She felt she was a portrait photographer by trade, working five days a week to make a living and spending only two days doing experimental work. Consequently, she said, her work was not well known.[99]

Coincidentally, one day after the *f.64* show opened, on November 16, 1932, Kanaga had an unsettling experience that had great impact on her life. As she and her sister, Neva, were riding in a car driven by the nineteen-year-old black youth Eluard Luchell McDaniel, they were stopped by two plainclothesmen (one a southerner), who took them to the Hall of Justice for questioning. The officers justified their action, saying that they were suspicious when they saw two white women in a car with a "negro" and intended to establish "unwritten Jim Crow laws in San Francisco regardless of California law." This story made the front page of *The San Francisco Chronicle* when Kanaga and her sister accused the police inspectors of "browbeating" them

Fig. 16. *Frances,* c. early 1930s
Gelatin silver toned print
$9^3/_4$ x $7^3/_4$
82.65.396

and McDaniel. The assistant district attorney stated that there were no Jim Crow laws in California, and under pressure from the mayor, the police inspectors publicly apologized to the women. McDaniel never received an apology, but his fingerprints were destroyed a week later.[100]

McDaniel had been living with the Kanaga family since Kanaga and an art critic, Junius Cravens, had found him on the beach in 1931.[101] The son of a fundamentalist preacher (who had beaten him once too often), McDaniel had hoboed his way to San Francisco, living off tips and handouts from the locals until Connie and Neva hired him as a houseboy and chauffeur. According to an interview with McDaniel years later, Kanaga adopted him as a houseboy, exchanging room and board for various jobs from sweeping the porch to helping out in the darkroom. She insisted that he go to school, and he eventually attended junior high, high school, and San Francisco State College. She also introduced him to union and leftist activities, bringing him to the International Longshoreman's Association, where he eventually became a union organizer. He claimed he assisted Kanaga in taking pictures during the San Francisco longshoremen's strike of 1934 and met many radical thinkers, including Lincoln Steffens and Ella Winters. He said of Kanaga, "She was a society photographer who has lost a lot of money customers because she was associated with radicals."[102]

McDaniel became one of Kanaga's favorite models during the early 1930s, and those pictures are undoubtedly among her very best. His sensuous, sculptural face was particularly arresting to her, and he was pliable as a model. The portraits are powerful and unsentimental, with a visceral quality unlike any other photographs of blacks done at that time. One picture of McDaniel lying down and pressing his hands to his face is particularly imaginative, revealing a free interaction between model and photographer (fig. 17). Kanaga painted with light to portray African Americans as people of beauty, inner strength, and unassailable dignity. Looking at Steichen's stunning portrait of Paul Robeson as the Emperor Jones, taken two years after Kanaga's major portraits of McDaniel, one wonders whether he had seen her work. Her portraits, including those of McDaniel and Kenneth Spencer (plates 35, 39) and *Frances with a Flower* (plate 30), are unique in their portrayal of blacks as individuals rather than stereotypes. At the time only the ethnic consciousness of black portrait photographers (notably, James Van Der Zee) equaled the sensitivity to ordinary black people found in Kanaga's work.

Fig. 19. Alma Lavenson
Consuelo Kanaga, c. 1933
Modern print from negative
Courtesy Alma Lavenson Associates
and Susan Ehrens

In June 1932 Langston Hughes, the African-American writer and poet, had come to Carmel, California, to visit Ella Winters, the wife of Lincoln Steffens. It was probably at this time that he made a side trip to San Francisco, where Kanaga (who knew Winters and Steffens) did some unusually striking portraits of him. Vintage copies of these photographs have yet to come to light, but the negatives exist (see plates 49, 50).

While Kanaga was busy with her work, her husband was growing restless. McCarthy, who had been wounded in World War I as a fighter pilot, finally had to have his right hand amputated. Unable to perform as an athlete and as a writer, he drank more and more, becoming increasingly abusive. Kanaga offered to help him buy a restaurant. With their friend Red Symes, he started a small hamburger joint off what was then Highway Camino Real in Belmont. McCarthy's great charm, along with his ability to trade on Kanaga's many wealthy friends, made it easy for him to borrow money freely. After accumulating a considerable sum, he disappeared. Kanaga was wild with grief. Her nephew, Chick (fig. 18), came to her rescue. Because she could not work or sleep, he plied her with an enormous amount of liquor, and when she had slept it off, she was cured of McCarthy.[103] It took her years to pay off his debts, but she honored them all. By 1934 she was listed in the San Francisco Directory under "Kanaga, photographer," with a studio on Montgomery Street.

While working in San Francisco in the early 1930s, Kanaga became more and more committed with radical activities on the West Coast. In October 1933 she became involved with a group called the Photo Commontors, along with Maynard Dixon, Dorothea Lange, Willard Van Dyke, Otto Hagel, Hansel Mieth, and Lester Balog (a founding member of the New York–based Film and Photo League). In May 1934 the first and only exhibition of Photo Commontors was held in the gallery at Gelber-Lilienthal Bookstore. The show, which included 100 photographs, was up for only a day before it was closed down by the objections of the American Legion.[104]

That month, on May 8, the San Francisco Longshoreman's Association began a strike led by Harry Bridges, which began in the Bay district, with ten marine craft tying up the entire shipping industry. On July 6 two strikers were killed and sixty-four hospitalized. By July 16, 150,000 workers walked out, only to be confronted two days later by 30,000 soldiers, police, and vigilantes.[105] Balog smuggled Kanaga into a *Western Worker* newspaper office "when it was busted up. She came in with an 8 x 10 camera."[106] A 1937 article presented Kanaga's recollections of the event: "She found herself in the midst of a riot. She saw policemen's clubs swinging in circles, a giant longshoreman

with a piece of fence felled three policemen. When she developed her film she had many double exposures, but two remarkable documents. One of the circular motion of the police clubs, the other of three policemen stretched out on the ground." "But for this experience I might still be doing quiet portraiture," she stated. "I was rudely awakened to the social scene. It now seemed to me the richest field for photography is history in the making, the rhythm and tragedy of the human struggle. Here are masterpieces to be made quite different from the posed photograph."[107]

During this period in California, Kanaga appears to have been self-employed as a portrait photographer, taking an occasional job as a stringer for *The San Francisco Chronicle* and the *San Francisco Daily News*. According to her nephew, Chick, she traveled often for commissions around the San Francisco area and was seldom home.[108]

In the winter of 1934 or early spring of 1935, Kanaga received an assignment to do a series on movie actors and actresses. Her nephew, Chick, drove her to the Metro-Goldwyn-Mayer studio in Los Angeles, where she photographed three subjects in one week. At the Beverly Hills estate of Harold Lloyd, the silent-film star, and his wife, Mildred Davis, she spent nine hours on the job and finally left in disgust. According to Amos and Chick, she found the movie stars phony, the entire idea bored her, and she quit the assignment.[109]

In the late spring of 1935, probably seeking magazine work or hoping to renew her contacts during the early Depression years, Kanaga returned to New York City. Her lifelong sensitivity to radical causes and the plight of the poor drew her to the Film and Photo League, a group of socially committed photographers. (In 1936 they split up to form the Film League, Photo League, and Frontier Films.) No formal records exist of when she actually joined, which may have been as early as 1931.[110]

Kanaga became very friendly with several members of the Photo League but did not involve herself with the petty, internecine politics that eventually tore apart the organization even before it was finally destroyed by the flood of anti-left feeling that swept the American political establishment in the fifties. Years later she spoke about the importance of joining: "The League was a completely new experience for me, a place for work and growth for young people without money. . . . It was a small helpful noncompetitive world."[111]

The photographers of the Photo League—including Lucy Ashjian, Harold Corsini, Morris Engel, Sid Grossman, Rosalie Gwathmey, Arthur Leipzig, Rebecca Lepkoff, Sol Libsohn, Jack Manning, Ruth Orkin, Aaron Siskind, W. Eugene Smith, Walter Rosenblum, Dan Weiner, and Max Yavno—at first promoted documentary photography but by the forties broadened their goals to include creative photography. Their early major projects, inspired by Berenice Abbott's three-year Works Progress Administration documentation of New York (published in 1939 as *Changing New York*), constitute the best-known photographic profile of New York and the handsomest. The Photo League enterprises included a three-year project headed by Aaron Siskind, "The Harlem Document," which was the most successful and significant examination of a black neighborhood ever attempted. Other League projects included "Pitt Street" (focusing on the Lower East Side) and "The Chelsea Document." It was "The Harlem Document" that attracted Kanaga's attention and prompted her to answer a questionnaire to work with Siskind and Yavno on a project to be called "The Most Crowded Block in the World"[112]—according to Siskind, "the block between 142nd Street and 143rd Street between Lenox and Seventh Avenues."[113]

Although Siskind did not remember hiring Kanaga to work on the project, it is difficult to determine the extent of her activities at the Photo League—possibly because of her own reticence on the subject coupled with the way some male associates like Siskind underestimated her contribution to the organization. Siskind remembered Kanaga as "sweet, lovely, darling, and I looked up to her as coming out of f.64, which stresses quality. I never saw many of her photographs. Connie loved black people." He added, "She was a 'fellow traveler' but did not belong to the Photo League."[114] (He was mistaken on both counts.) It is possible that Siskind and Kanaga photographed together during the mid-1930s. Both took photographs of the May Day Parade in Union Square—he in 1936, she in 1937 (fig. 20)—and four of her photographs were featured in *Direction* magazine in May of the following year.

The Photo League's newsletter, *Photo Notes*, indicates Kanaga's activities in 1938–39: on February 7, 1938, she lectured at the League with Siskind, discussing documentary and feature photography; from February to May 1938, she ran a feature group, "Neighborhoods of New York," which met three times a month; from December to January 1939, she held an "illustrative group," which met at her studio once a week and contributed regularly to exhibitions (see plate 2, fig. 22); and in February 1939 she was part

Fig. 22. [*Tenements*] (New York), mid–late 1930s
Gelatin silver toned print
9 1/2 x 7 1/4
82.65.38

Fig. 23. Cover of *Labor Defender*
(January 1936)
Estate of Wallace B. Putnam

of a committee for an exhibition of photography to be held at the World's Fair (which did not come to pass).

Kanaga was a good friend of Max Yavno, whom she must have met when he and Siskind were roommates in 1935 and 1936.[115] She remembered Yavno as "one I went photographing with to show the merits of the larger camera. Yavno was a 35mm man."[116] In the 1970s Yavno spoke of her fondly but was dismissive of her technique and noted that she was "romantically involved with politics": "Kanaga knew almost nothing technical about photography, but was poetic and beautiful. Her portraits were great. They were her forte."[117]

Max Yavno only admitted his debt to Kanaga three years after her death, in his recollections included in Ben Maddow's *Photography of Max Yavno:* "[Yavno's] real professional training came by watching his friend Consuelo Kanaga in the darkroom. He met her at the New York Photo League. . . . Her radical bent was almost entirely emotional. She was older, more sophisticated, . . . and lived in the expensive outskirts of the Village . . . . She knew little about lenses, but would print marvelously; could easily spend a week with one 4 x 5 negative. She taught Max Yavno . . . to distinguish between various shades of white in different grades of illustration board." When asked by Maddow, "Did you have any critical sense toward your work?" Yavno replied, " I remember Consuelo Kanaga sort of building up my ego. . . . And then I'd get too cocky, and she'd tear me down. And then she would build me up again."[118]

Another friend from the Photo League was Jack Manning (now a staff photographer for *The New York Times*), who was hired by Siskind to work on "The Harlem Document." He recalled that Kanaga reminded him of Margaret Bourke-White, "very beautiful and self-effacing at first meeting, very modest and introverted," but he noted that "she knew what she wanted to do irrespective of circumstance." She was more than twenty-five years older than the eighteen-year-old Manning, but at no time did he notice an age gap. She had "a sparkling personality" and made him feel unselfconscious, but he was put off, he said, by her drinking problem. They dated briefly but "were never intimate." He recalled a time when Kanaga was teaching Max Yavno how to take a picture of a rooster (see plate 3). Manning was surprised to learn that Kanaga had gotten married in 1936; with characteristic mystery, she had never mentioned it.[119]

In 1935–36, while she was involved with the Photo League, Kanaga was also photographing for *New Masses, Daily Worker* and *Sunday Worker, Labor Defender* (fig. 23), and other radical periodicals; in 1936 she took a course on "Fundamentals of Marxism" at the Workers School at 35 East Twelfth Street.[120]

Kanaga's most important project at the time, she said years later, was her series of photographs of a young African-American widow, Annie Mae Merriweather, which appeared in *New Masses* in 1935 (plate 4). Kanaga became fascinated by Merriweather's beauty and courage after photographing her several times. Merriweather's husband, Jim Press Merriweather, had been lynched while trying to form a sharecroppers' union in Lowndes County, Alabama. She herself had also been beaten and tortured.[121]

LEFT
Fig. 24. *Two Women, Harlem*, mid–late 1930s
Gelatin silver toned print
9⁷/₈ x 11³/₄
82.65.424

RIGHT
Fig. 25. *Girl at Easter* (New York), mid–late
1930s
9⁷/₈ x 7⁵/₈
82.65.461

Edward Steichen, who included the Merriweather portrait in his exhibition *50 Photographs by 50 Photographers* at The Museum of Modern Art in 1948, said of the work: "Look at that face. All the turmoil and suffering of oppression is captured in that one picture and yet it's a most simple subject."[122] The photograph came into the possession of Carl Gustav Jung around the time of the exhibition through Walter Lewisohn, a patron of Kanaga's. Lewisohn's sister wrote to Kanaga of Jung's "great delight with the picture referred to as the 'Black Madonna,'" saying he wanted to know something more of this woman, "her background, her problems, what lies behind those eyes?"[123]

In 1936 Kanaga became interested in focusing on a portfolio of "Negro studies" that would reflect "what experience and appreciation I have for these beautiful people." She began looking for a place in Harlem where she could find models and "half decent conditions for work"; she wanted to live with a "Negro family" and had the addresses of some "good Christian" families from the Harlem YWCA. "Why wasn't I born black, I would have loved it so?" she wrote Bender.[124] It is probable that she did move in with two young black women for a few months in the mid- to late 1930s while keeping her studio at 15 West Ninth Street (see figs. 24, 25).[125]

In February 1936 an assignment Kanaga was carrying out for the arts program of the WPA led to an encounter that altered the course of her personal life. In connection with her work on the Index of American Design, she was sent to 59 Morton Street in Greenwich Village to photograph a mantelpiece in a house that had allegedly once belonged to the nineteenth-century department-store magnate A. T. Stewart. She had been "warned that 'there was a crazy artist' who worked at night and slept all day living in the studio where she would find the mantelpiece. She was advised not to disturb

Fig. 26. Marjorie Content
Consuelo Kanaga
3³/₄ x 2⁷/₈
Collection of Susan Sandberg

Fig. 27. *Wally*, mid-1930s
Gelatin silver toned print
9⁵/₈ x 5¹/₁₆
Estate of Wallace B. Putnam

him but when she entered and found him asleep, she turned her camera on him."[126] Kanaga described the meeting to Bender: "It was a startling experience to me upon first entering his studio—a large rather empty room with stacks of paintings, rather strange ones—and one huge mask six feet high [called *Agog*] and a face made with every sort of an object from a mousetrap, false hair—down to baby shoes."[127]

She had met the artist once before, in 1931, through her best friend, Marjorie Content, a writer and photographer (fig. 26).[128] At the time Content had been married to Harold Loeb, who was the owner of the avant-garde Sunwise Turn Bookshop at 51 East Forty-fourth Street and also published a literary magazine called *Broom*. The Loebs attracted many literary and artistic people, including Hugo Robus, Henry Varnum Poor, Georgia O'Keeffe, Mark Rothko, Milton Avery, and Wallace Putnam. Many of the artists were from the "New City" group.[129]

Wallace Bradstreet Putnam, a mildly eccentric, handsome artist and writer, lived with his aunt and uncle at 59 Morton Street (fig. 27). For many years he had been a friend and confidant of Marjorie Content. He was a rather shy young man and intensely self-centered. Immersed in Eastern religions, he led a relatively ascetic existence, at one point spending some months living in a cave at the foot of the Palisades in New Jersey. He worked nights for *The Sun* as a retoucher and artist and, despite his handsome looks, did not actively seek the companionship of single women. Older married women made him feel more at ease.[130] The encounter in 1936 was a success. Kanaga fell in love again.

She was forty-two years old, five years older than Putnam. Years later he recalled, "[We] shared an essential view of life. . . . We differed in that she as a woman wanted to feed the physically hungry first, while I felt that humanity's spiritual need was primary. I was driven to get to God. She knew the ultimate uselessness of that drive but maybe underestimated the usefulness of striving."[131] Kanaga never made a public statement about their marriage one way or the other.

Shortly after they met, on May 8, 1936, Putnam wrote to his good friend Jean Toomer, "Found a nice place on Staten Island for Aunt and Uncle who move next Saturday so won't be long before Connie will be here at 59 Morton." He added, "We're considering your suggestion of solemnizing our being together."[132]

Marjorie Content and Jean Toomer were among the couple's best friends. Content, already a photographer when she met Kanaga, learned much through their friendship. She was one of the few people in whom Kanaga confided besides Bender. Putnam identified strongly with the philosophy and character of Jean Toomer, who was a major influence on black writers of the Harlem Renaissance. Toomer's best-known written work was his semiautobiographical novel, *Cane* (1923). He was a follower of the Russian mystic Georges Gurdjieff until his marriage to Content in 1934, at which time he turned to Quakerism.[133] Kanaga and Putnam became regular visitors to the Toomers' home in Doylestown, Pennsylvania. The Toomers also introduced them to the Taos art and literary colony led by Mabel Dodge Luhan and her circle of friends, including Frieda Lawrence and Dorothy Brett. Both Putnam and Kanaga already knew Georgia O'Keeffe—he, through Milton and Sally Avery and she, through Litchfield and Stieglitz.

The Averys, who had known Putnam long before they met Kanaga, became close friends of the pair. Along with Jean Toomer and Marjorie Content, they attended the couple's marriage on May 28, 1936, in the Municipal Building near City Hall in downtown Manhattan. Sally Avery remarked of the marriage, "Strange that she should end up with someone as puritanical as Wally."[134]

The couple set off for their honeymoon on a farm in Vermont owned by a couple named Stanley. The husband was Putnam's boss on *The Sun*. Kanaga took a photograph of the Stanleys, posing them as the quintessential American farm owners, which she called *The Front Parlor* (plate 66). It was used to illustrate a short story in *Direction* magazine for March–April 1939.

On their way to Vermont, the Putnams stopped at Lake George to visit with Stieglitz. Kanaga used the opportunity to photograph her mentor and friend (fig. 28). They also visited New Hampshire and stayed with Putnam's sister Florence and her new husband, the artist Ralph McClellen, in Rockport, Massachusetts.

Kanaga moved to 59 Morton Street with Putnam, who at that time was working for *The Sun* at night. Kanaga was involved with the Photo League during the day. The pair probably did not see much of each other for several years. However, in 1937 Kanaga's mother suffered a stroke, and Kanaga took this occasion to bring her husband home to her family in San Francisco for a brief visit.

The early years with her third husband were sometimes difficult for Kanaga, although she was grateful to have found him. She told a close friend that he could be wonderful, saying, "I don't even enjoy an ice cream alone without Wally," and confided he had rescued her from the anguish of her former marriage. This romantic idea may have helped her through the

Fig. 28. *Stieglitz at Lake George*, 1936
8¼ x 6½
82.65.213

adjustment period, but not entirely. On occasion she found it necessary to leave Putnam for short periods to stay with friends.[135]

Putnam introduced Kanaga to Krishnamurti's Vedanta Society, which they attended for two years between the late 1930s and 1940. Kanaga became interested in Eastern philosophy, according to Putnam, through her father, although sometimes, according to a friend, she would get "fed up with all that Zen stuff."[136]

Between 1938 and 1954, Kanaga free-lanced for several women's magazines, primarily *Woman's Day*, for which she produced photographs for some sixty articles. The society and children's portraiture that she had been doing independently had taught her how to popularize her imagery. She was an immediate success at magazine illustration, and within a year or two, she was able to support herself and her husband on magazine work alone.

Putnam wrote to Jean Toomer and Marjorie Content in 1941 that Kanaga was "discouraged, sickened at times doing this magazine work."[137] While working on such articles as "How We Like Boys to Act on a Date" and "Mothers Need to Be Hardy Souls," she was also photographing for *Labor Defender, World Magazine, Direction*, and *New Masses*. Surely she enjoyed the assignments for the leftist magazines, but she must have derived some pleasure and satisfaction from the commercial work, as well. Kanaga chose to invest her meager funds in a Zeiss Jewel camera in 1941 for her commercial magazine work. It is also notable that one of her photographs for *Woman's Day* appeared as an illustration of exemplary work in *A Guide to Better Photography*, by Berenice Abbott.[138]

With the extra money from Kanaga's magazine work, the Putnams were able to improve their standard of living and moved several times. From Morton Street they moved to Eighth Street, next door to the old Whitney Museum, and then to a loft on Eighteenth Street, off Gramercy Park (fig. 30), where they lived for at least two years. Finally they found an apartment on Cornelia Street.[139] Putnam, however, had always wanted a place in the country. In 1940 Kirk Wilkinson, who employed Kanaga as a free-lance photographer for *Woman's Day*, sold them some land with a pond and an old icehouse in Yorktown Heights near Croton-on-Hudson, in Westchester County. As Putnam remembered it: "There must have been three feet of sawdust on the ground and a couple of walls were pretty much gone. We came out here with a tent on weekends to see if we would like it."[140] When they bought it in 1940 for ten dollars, they had only fifty dollars in the bank.

Between 1937 and 1940, there were continuing signs of strain in the marriage. Kanaga's next trip to San Francisco was taken alone; it may have been her intention to get away from her marriage for a little while. Putnam wrote her: "I'm so glad you're coming home, so glad you're feeling better, if I can be a proper husband to you it will be enough." He went on to deplore his constant concern about painting, admitting, "I take myself so damned seriously,"[141] but a later letter is consumed with talk of his work.

By 1945 Putnam began to press for spending more time at the Icehouse. Kanaga was reluctant: her resistance prompted a letter from her husband, the tenor of which suggests that their marriage had become delicately balanced: "Dear Connie, I want you to be . . . happy and at ease and

LEFT
Fig. 29. Max Yavno
Consuelo Kanaga and Wallace Putnam
4 x 5
Estate of Wallace B. Putnam

RIGHT
Fig. 30. *Interior of Kanaga's Studio*
Modern print from negative
82.65.1982

working (photographing) and if we go to the Icehouse now, let us make it a point not to become involved—let us go there now only with the idea of trying to get the place cleaner, more convenient and comfortable . . . and if we find ourselves getting involved . . . and miserable, let us get out. Your happiness is important to me. . . . You apparently are being shaken terribly by the roots. . . . Let us trust life more and this Great Self of the world . . . our Self."[142]

They began to spend five months in the city and seven months at the Icehouse. Putnam would get home from the newspaper at three or four in the morning. Kanaga would paint at night. She had also learned to play the recorder from Marjorie Content and in turn taught Putnam. It afforded her much comfort. She became increasingly adept at it and taught many of her friends to play.[143]

Kanaga was distressed that she had less time to pursue her own work in her studio. Each time she left to visit her family or stay with a friend, Putnam wrote her letters of reassurance, urging her to "accept herself as she is, the good with the bad, identifying with neither side . . . seeing both the negative and positive realities, and knowing them for what they are . . . [for] out of such an experience can come a central peace." In another letter he entreated: "It seems that we can love life, love this world, adore it, wonder at it, enjoy it. BUT ON CONDITION THAT WE LOVE ALL OF IT." He begged her to "find joy in life helping each other," ending his letter, "The badness in us is part of the picture too."[144]

These letters betray themselves as somewhat manipulative and point to problems that are never clearly defined. One thing is certain from interviews with Kanaga's friends and from her own words: she detested hypocrisy and could never tolerate any form of pomposity or pretense.

The year 1948 was an outstanding one for Kanaga. Her technique had fully matured, and her work was included in three major exhibitions. Three of her abstractions (plates 109, 111, 112), experiments with water and light made at the Icehouse pond, appeared in an exhibition that opened in April at The Museum of Modern Art called *In and Out of Focus*. The exhibition, organized by Edward Steichen and containing 185 images, showed the work of fifty-five photographers, including Berenice Abbott, Ansel Adams, Richard Avedon, Henri Cartier-Bresson, Walker Evans, Maya Elanore Deren, Helen Levitt, Barbara Morgan, Paul Strand, Aaron Siskind, and Gordon Parks. At Phillips Academy in Andover, Massachusetts, *Photographic Pioneers*, opening at the Addison Gallery of American Art in late May, was a series of shows including 250 works by Atget lent by Berenice Abbott; 100 photographs by Cartier-Bresson; and works using imagery that was experimental in interpretation and technique by nineteen contemporary photographers including Kanaga, Berenice Abbott, Lotte Jacobi, Ernst Halberstadt, Harry Callahan, Charles Sheeler, Andreas Feininger, and others. Kanaga's works (plates 109, 111, 112) were contrasted with those of Francis Bruguière (coincidentally, a San Francisco photographer whose work Kanaga had admired early in her career): his abstract imagery turned reality into fantasy, while her apparently fantastical images were actually reflections in the Icehouse pond. Finally, *50 Photographs by 50 Photographers*, an abbreviated history of photography at The Museum of Modern Art, organized by Edward Steichen, included one image from Kanaga's series of Annie Mae Merriweather.[145]

Kanaga had often voiced the desire to "make a portfolio of Negro studies."[146] For years she had promised herself that she would go to the South and photograph as long as she could afford to stay there.[147] Her marriage to Putnam and the work of restoring the Icehouse in its final phase had intervened, but at last she felt free to go. It was probably in the spring of 1948 that Kanaga took a trip to Tennessee. While it cannot be determined why she went there or with whom she stayed (possibly Louise Dahl-Wolfe, whose husband had family there), she produced some of her most powerful photographs of African Americans (plates 81, 83, 84).

She must have been distressed to learn in 1950 that *The Sun* had folded and Putnam had resolved that they should move to the Icehouse permanently.[148] At first Kanaga refused. Putnam, who intended to devote himself entirely to painting, promised to build her an adequate darkroom. She could work for *Woman's Day*, and he would sell his paintings. Somewhat reluctantly, Kanaga finally agreed to move.

With the help of her nephew, Chick, who had been working to fix up the Icehouse, a makeshift darkroom was constructed. Tiny (three by seven feet) and with almost no ventilation, it remained Kanaga's darkroom for the rest of her life. Isolated from the city, she began to seek subjects in her home and used the grounds at the Icehouse in her photography (see fig. 58, p. 144).

Kanaga worked to make the best of her marriage at the Icehouse. Before she married Putnam, she had not been "much of a household manager,"[149] but by 1950 she had become a superb cook. She bought a huge red Garland cooking stove, collected agate ware and pewter utensils, and baked bread. Every time she passed her red stove, though, she gave it a hearty kick.[150]

To all of her neighbors along Baptist Church Road and many of her patrons, who were impressed with her gift as an enchanting storyteller and her ability to listen, the marriage of this oddly matched couple was a mystery. Kanaga was alternately amused and exasperated by her husband's preoccupation with his painting. Any visitor who came to see her was swiftly whisked away to view Putnam's work. Amid his lengthy explication, Kanaga would occasionally interject a comment in her gravelly voice, once muttering quietly while he was displaying some paintings of Christ, "Why does Jesus Christ always end up looking like Wallace Putnam?"[151]

During the winter of 1949–50, Milton and Sally Avery invited Putnam and Kanaga to stay with them at an artists' colony in Maitland, Florida, near Orlando. The Research Studio was a six-acre complex with tiny studios and a communal dining hall. Sally Avery recalls that Kanaga spent the first month in bed reading mystery stories. She eventually did go out to black baseball games and to a revivalist church near Maitland and shared community dinners with artists like Boris Margo, Arnold Blanche, and Doris Lee. Finally her mood changed, and she took some fifty photographs of Milton Avery, which she planned to print when she returned to the Icehouse.[152] More important, she went to the "mucklands," the fields of a reclaimed swampy area outside Maitland where migrant workers were picking crops of early lettuce and other vegetables. It was there that she made a series of pictures, including her best-known image, *She Is a Tree of Life to Them,* a portrait of a tall, thin black woman with her two small children, a boy and a girl, standing in the shelter of her arms (plate 90, fig. 31). Steichen gave the portrait this title (Proverbs 3:18) when he included it in his landmark exhibition, *The Family of Man,* in 1955. Kanaga later said that Steichen, when asked on television to choose his favorite photograph from the exhibition, held up the catalogue to show her powerful portrait, saying, "This is it." She went on to say that the monumental composition was "influenced by the work of Sargent Johnson, a black sculptor she knew in San Francisco whom she greatly admired."[153]

In the same interview, she described how she came to photograph this mother with her children: "I had made some photographs of her . . . and her husband liked them . . . [and] he said he didn't know she was so good looking. She worked with her husband in the Mucklands. She was seeing me off when I was leaving. . . . I saw this potential for a beautiful photograph. And I asked her to draw the little boy closer and the little girl closer. I had her move . . . so she had this cement wall in back of her. . . . It's the most—liked photograph I've ever taken."

After leaving Florida, en route to New York, Kanaga and Putnam went back to Tennessee. There Kanaga took a series of striking photographs of the black sculptor William Edmondson (plate 94, fig 32).

For the most part, from 1951 to 1963 Kanaga probably devoted her photographic activities to making a living through commercial portraiture. She charged only ten dollars per portrait, which meant she had to spend most of her time in the darkroom. Putnam did some teaching and sold his paintings occasionally, and they rented out the Icehouse every summer, which produced a minimal income. It is hardly surprising that Kanaga made so few images of her own choosing during this period.

In August 1952 Kanaga and Putnam went to California and on the way back stopped off in Taos. Kanaga spent time with her friend and patron

Walter (Buddy) Lewisohn, who was shooting a movie about the Navajo Indians. According to Lewisohn's wife, Florence, "Connie got balky about taking pictures of the Navajo, insisting that it would be intrusive to take advantage of their privacy" (see plates 67–70).[154] The couple was in Taos on May 27, 1953, when they received word that Kanaga's mother had died; they subsequently returned to California to attend the funeral.

By early August Steichen asked Kanaga, who was back in Taos, to be in the *Family of Man* exhibition.[155] In late November 1954 he requested the negatives of the prints he intended to use: *She Is a Tree of Life to Them* and an image of a young black girl taken in Tennessee in 1948. Kanaga, who prided herself on her printing, was probably somewhat taken aback to discover that the photographs were to be enlarged and printed by the museum. She was sixty-one when the exhibition opened in January 1955, and it was the most recognition she had received in the previous six years.

The Putnams spent the summer of 1955 in Maine, and in 1956 they visited Grand Manan Island, off the coast of New Brunswick, Canada, stopping off on their way home to spend time with Marjorie Content and Jean Toomer in Doylestown. It was to Content that Kanaga years later confided the horrors of her second marriage and the debts that McCarthy had saddled her with, concluding: "If it meant anything to me[,] in time it might be the necessity of complete faith in one's companion and thank God Wal is different. Life is unpredictable and has its way of growing us. Looking back, I can't regret it. It seems I had to get knocked about for every tiny bit of growth. I could not give up anything, the good or bads or soft or hards. The understandings from even the darkest days have such precious value."[156]

On a trip to Taos in 1958, she took a few fine pictures of Navajo and Hopi children (plate 27). She still would not let herself take pictures of adults freely because of her respect for their privacy; she talked often about taking pictures of Native Americans with Walter Lewisohn, but each time she tried, she became overwhelmed and froze.[157] Instead, Kanaga concentrated mainly on children, with whom she could always form an easy rapport.

In the winter of 1962, the Lewisohns offered Kanaga and Putnam the use of their house on the island of St. Croix in exchange for minding their two children while they went to Peru for two months. The experience convinced Kanaga and Putnam that parenting would never have worked for them.[158] The following year they returned to St. Croix and this trip produced several fine photographs of native children, including *School Girl* (plate 28).

In January 1964 Kanaga was invited to make a nine-day visit to Albany, Georgia, where she photographed and lived with a group of eighteen young men and women, white and black (mostly college students). It would be her last opportunity to photograph the kind of subjects that inspired her most. The group, which called itself the Quebec-Washington-Guantánamo Walk for Peace, had walked through Canada and the United States on their way to Cuba, carrying placards and leaflets with a message of peace and integration. Kanaga's friend the poet Barbara Deming (fig. 35) persuaded her to bring along her camera to record the event. Kanaga wrote to Marjorie Content of her adventure: "I went to Albany, Georgia, last month to photograph the Peace Walkers. They had just gotten out of jail and a long fast. I stayed until they tried to walk again and were arrested. There was no brutality but what a strange atmosphere . . . a white prison and a black prison."[159]

LEFT
Fig. 33. Alma Lavenson
Imogen Cunningham, Alma Lavenson,Consuelo Kanaga, c. 1952
5 x 5³/₈
Estate of Wallace B. Putnam; Alma Lavenson Associates and Susan Ehrens

RIGHT
Fig. 34. Imogen Cunningham (?)
Connie Smoking, c. 1952
7⁹/₁₆ x 6
Estate of Wallace B. Putnam, Courtesy of Kristina Amadeus

Fig. 35. *Barbara Deming*
9³/₄ x 7⁵/₈
82.65.454

Kanaga lived with the marchers in the black section of town and attended a black church with some of them. She said of the experience, "I stood on the street as they began their walk . . . and began to tremble." As they approached the waiting police, "I felt the terror of seeing a lot of white men but no one who looked kindly."[160] Kanaga took a few photographs, some of which were used in Deming's book, *Prison Notes* (1966). She also made some friends, among them the peace activist Ray Robinson (fig. 43).

After years of urging from his wife, Putnam in 1964 finally decided that he was ready to travel to Europe. The couple spent several months at a house lent by friends in Lacoste, France, an area in Provence favored by artists.[161] Kanaga, who at seventy-three had developed emphysema and had lost the strength to work as she wished, mostly made contact prints of her visits to Lacoste (she and Putnam returned there in 1967). Her photographs, especially the landscapes, indicate that her work had lost none of its beauty and power; the skill was there but not the stamina (fig. 36).

On May 16, 1968, Kanaga entered Northern Westchester Hospital for an operation for colon cancer. Once again her nephew came from California to nurse her. He built a separate studio behind the Icehouse where he could stay while she recuperated. Eventually it became Putnam's studio, where he painted and slept.

As she recovered slowly, Kanaga would drag herself into her darkroom to work on a print, sometimes taking as long as five hours to get the effect she wanted. Her stamina and will to continue a normal existence were extraordinary.

The following year, in 1969, a patron and friend of Kanaga and Putnam's, the collector and real estate magnate Alexander Simon Bing (fig. 37), died. An amateur photographer, he left Kanaga much of his photographic equipment, including an enlarger to replace the outdated and faulty one she had used for more than thirty years. In his will he bequeathed Kanaga and Putnam the sum of $2,000 each. This seemed like an enormous amount of money to them; they had managed on so little that they feared the extra money would upset the balance of their frugal way of life. Kanaga wrote to Marjorie Content, "Probably in time we will know how to use it."[162]

Kanaga spent the remainder of her life advising young photographers who came to visit her, taking photographs of the children of her friends and neighbors, and printing, on rare occasions when she could find the strength. She made a few experiments in color photography with a 35mm camera but never printed them. None of them were portraits. In 1973–74 she photographed and printed her last noncommercial portrait, of W. Eugene Smith and his wife, Aileen (fig. 47).

Her comfort came from those friends and neighbors who cherished her eccentricities as well as her purity of spirit. She was universally considered to be without pretense of any kind. Self-effacing but with a bitter edge to her tongue, she remained loyal in her own fashion to her husband from the day she moved into the Icehouse. Putnam came first with her, as friends and acquaintances have noted: "[She felt that] her work wasn't important. His work was important."[163]

The recollections of the photography historian and dealer Helen Gee

Left

Fig. 36. *Stairs* (Lacoste, France), mid-1960s
Modern print from negative
82.65.771

Right

Fig. 37. *Alexander Bing*
4⁷/₈ x 3³/₄
82.65.67

are especially revealing: "I wanted to show Consuelo's work in the late 1950s at the *Limelight* [Gee's gallery]. I arranged with a friend to drive me up to her house. . . . As soon as we got there, she insisted that we eat and afterwards I asked to see her photographs. She proceeded to wander around the house looking for them in an aimless fashion. She couldn't seem to focus at all. She couldn't find the photographs. The conclusion was that Wally began to show us his canvases of two birds. . . . There must have been two hundred canvases. . . . So, she never had a show. I didn't see one photograph and it didn't seem to bother her at all."[164]

In the 1970s Kanaga's work was recognized in two retrospectives and two solo exhibitions (see Chronology). Nevertheless, in her last years she seems to have lost the will to fight. One friend commented: "Toward the end she felt a dissatisfaction with life. Wally had a certain vanity. Connie's last years were frustrated." Another noted that at the end of her life Kanaga was no longer interested in people.[165]

Before Kanaga died, two young collectors, Harvey S. S. Miller and J. Randall Plummer, one of them (Plummer) a photographer, came to buy a few prints by her and by other artists whose work she had accumulated over the years: "She was dead broke. She hadn't the strength left to print her scratched and neglected negatives." She spoke of her own work as "a search for luminosity, the glow on petals, the curve of flesh." She talked of African Americans only in these terms, as sculptural and beautiful. When they looked at her set of *Camera Work* autographed by Stieglitz, they discovered she had paid $200 in the 1920s. When Stieglitz asked her at the time, "How can you afford to buy this?" she told them that she replied, "This is my millinery."[166]

Fig. 38. Judith Kalina
Consuelo Kanaga, 1971
7 x 5
Courtesy of Judith Kalina

Toward the end of her life, Kanaga, in an introspective mood, made some written observations that seem to summarize her conflicts and character best:

Am I a poor taker? Why? What do I want?

Am I concealing my needs and yearnings? Why should I insist on being second and carry resentments for years?

Why really have I not driven the car? Is it to shackle myself and suffer more? Why do I look down on money as an evil and yet be in need of enough to live on?

Was it necessary to divide my creative work so called which aims at reality—with portrait work which I feel must be softened and flattering? Aren't they one?

Why have I turned away from thinking about what to eat!!! Sometimes I make Wallace suggest what we might eat. To make him pay?

Why have I felt shut in at the Icehouse—when it is so beautiful and I am so fond of the plantings etc.?

What do I lack in physical needs? Clothes? Food? Shelter?

Would cutting off my hair free me of any strings or bonds?

Do I want to die or be in jail again to be reborn — must one always become a captive to know freedom?

What am I—a mess or something reaching toward light?[167]

Kanaga's power as a photographer lay in her almost mystical belief that photography itself was a sacred trust, and in trying to fulfill that trust, she created some of the most sensitive works ever done in black portraiture. As she observed, "One thing I had to say in my photography was that Negroes are beautiful and that poverty is a tender and terrible subject to be approached on one's knees."[168]

Her high standards were reflected in every subject she chose to photograph, whether portraiture, abstraction, landscape, still life, journalism, or commercial photography. Her body of work, though comparatively small, was consistently fine. It was fine because she worked very hard for perfection and thus made very few prints. She chose to work alone, in keeping with her independent American pioneer spirit, insisting on doing her own printing and not seeking advice or recognition from her colleagues. She had no gift for self-promotion. Few people saw her work, and the consequence is the story of her career.

Consuelo Kanaga died at the age of eighty-three on February 28, 1978. When the time came for her to die, her body was worn out. She had suffered calamitous insults to her system brought on by the chemicals she chose to use to produce her superb prints, by the incessant smoking that calmed her nerves, and possibly by early alchohol abuse. However, her enormous and truthful spirit never wavered for a moment. She kept her artistic values and temperament and forced her skill until it could no longer sustain her.

In the end, only her fiercely loyal friends knew Kanaga's incredible capacity to keep working. Only a few of her marvelous photographs had entered the art market. She died virtually unknown, probably by her own choosing. During her entire life, her work appeared in only sixteen exhibitions, and only six of those were devoted to her photographs exclusively. Her productivity was comparatively limited, but that was also a choice she had made.

At her death, her entire estate amounted to $1,345 in photographic equipment, almost 2,500 negatives, and 375 prints; everything else of value was given away to her friends.

NOTES

Epigraphs: Blue Moon/Lerner-Heller 1974, p. 17.

1. Jean Therrier to Wallace Putnam, February 3, 1978, WPE. She continues: "Is it she who lives through us or we who live through her?"

2. Unless otherwise indicated, information and quotations concerning Kanaga's childhood have been drawn from Kenega Genealogy and autobiographical notes and personal observations by CK in Blue Moon/Lerner-Heller 1974, pp. 3–4, 16–17.

3. Kanaga's mother turned her home into a boarding house to support her children while their peripatetic father was on the road (telephone interview with Chick Brown by BHM, July 13, 1991). Judith Kalina remembers speaking to Louise Dahl-Wolfe, who said that Kanaga's father was a dreamer and her mother, the practical one (interview with Judith Kalina by SML, May 31, 1991). Another source of income was the money Amos senior occasionally made by selling parcels of land he had bought in Astoria, Oregon; New Mexico; and Arizona (telephone interview with Amos Kanaga, Jr., by BHM, June 25, 1991; interview with Wallace Putnam by SML, September 16, 1988).

4. Telephone interview with Amos Kanaga, Jr., by BHM, June 25, 1991; interview with Chick Brown by SML, October 7, 1988.

5. Wallace Putnam, quoted in Frankel 1978. In later years, according to Putnam, the only newspaper to which Kanaga subscribed regularly was *Fortune News*, a monthly published by ex-convicts. The plight of the prisoner remained important to her for the rest of her life (interview with Wallace Putnam by SML, September 16, l988).

6. Interview with Amos Kanaga, Jr., by BHM, March 25, 1991. According to a storytelling tape made by Kanaga, WPE, Neva would tell enchanting fairy stories and hint that she visited with a fairy prince at night and danced with him at balls. She kept Connie in her thrall by suggesting that Connie could come along only if she became a virtual slave to Neva. Neva knew magic and set tasks for Connie that would prove her capacity to believe. Connie would invariably fail to pass Neva's tests. This is one of many stories often repeated by Kanaga.

7. Interview with Winn Smith by BHM and SML, February 3, 1990.

8. The diary is in WPE.

9. Interview with March Avery by BHM and SML, February 20, 1990.

10. Mitchell 1979, p. 158.

11. Quoted in Frankel 1978.

12. Mitchell 1979, p. 159.

13. Riess 1968, pp. 87–88.

14. Telephone interview with Mrs. John R. Harrison by BHM, May 30, 1991.

15. Mitchell 1979, p. 159.

16. Telephone interview with Amos Kanaga, Jr., by BHM, March 25, 1991; interview with Amos Kanaga, Jr., by SML, March 31, 1990.

17. Information about Evans Davidson based on interview with Wallace Putnam by SML, September 16, 1988; and telephone interviews with Amos Kanaga, Jr., by BHM, March 25, 1991; and with Chick Brown by BHM, October 14, 1991.

18. Telephone interview with Amos Kanaga, Jr., by BHM, March 25, 1991.Before then, he and Connie had shared space in their parents' house at 4228 Twenty-sixth Street. She had used half a room to develop her pictures, and he had used the other half for his ham-radio operation. Amos remembered that he later wired her Post Street studio in 1924, when he was only fifteen.

19. Mitchell 1979, p. 159.

20. Mitchell 1979, p. 159.

21. Dahl-Wolfe Scrapbook 1984, p. 6.

22. Interview with Wallace Putnam by SML, September 16, 1988. Her newspaper job may have been with the *Rocky Mountain News* (see Bates 1976).

23. Undated storytelling tape, WPE. In 1926 Albert Bender made Kanaga a gift of Arnold Genthe's *Impressions of Old New Orleans*, a book of photographs taken in New Orleans about the same time she was there. (The book is part of the WPE.)

24. Note in WPE.

25. Mrs. Hearst's favorite charity was the "Milk Fund" for needy infants.

26. Unpublished interview with CK by Margaretta Mitchell, December 11, 1977, p. 7, Margaretta Mitchell personal archives.

27. Mitchell 1979, pp. 159–60.

28. Information in this essay concerning Donald Litchfield is culled from correspondence from Litchfield to Alfred Stieglitz between September 21, 1917, and August 10, 1929, Stieglitz Papers. "She met and fell in love. . .": Litchfield, Aldershot Camp, Nova Scotia, to Stieglitz, September 21, 1917; "somewhere in France," February 12, 1918; Hotel Pennsylvania, July 8, 1922.

29. Litchfield to Stieglitz, March 28, 1923. In New York Kanaga and Litchfield moved often, as was the custom in the twenties and thirties, when landlords offered rent bonuses to new tenants. Their address in November 1923 was a room on Waverly Place. About then, Litchfield wrote Stieglitz that Kanaga was thinking of "attending the Clarence White School" (Litchfield to Stieglitz, November 22, 1923).

30. Litchfield to Stieglitz, undated [winter 1922; incorrectly catalogued as April 1922].

31. Litchfield to Stieglitz, September 21, 1917; April 8, 1920; May 15, 1922; January 23, March 9, April 4, and May 18, 1923; April 24, July 30, August 3, and August 22, 1925; October 11, 1926.

32. Litchfield to Stieglitz, undated (letter begins: "My Dear Mr. Stieglitz, the all knowing 'one'").

33. Kanaga's tiny apartment on Bedford Street near the southwest corner of Christopher Street was in a narrow four-story brick and brownstone row house. It is unlikely that she would have established a usable studio in this apartment.

34. CK to Alfred Stieglitz, January 13, 1923, June 6, 1924, and undated, Stieglitz Papers.

35. Litchfield to Stieglitz, July 8, 1924.

36. Litchfield to Stieglitz, July 15, 1924.

37. Litchfield to Stieglitz, July 30, 1924.

38. Litchfield to Stieglitz, February 1, 1925; February 19, 1925.

39. Litchfield to Stieglitz, April 3, 1925.

40. Litchfield to Stieglitz, August 3, 1925.

41. Litchfield to Stieglitz, August 10, 1929.

42. Born in Dublin in 1866, the son of an Irish rabbi, Bender had come to the United States in 1883. After making his fortune in insurance and shipping, he had become a trustee of Mills College, commissioner of the San Francisco Public Library, and director of the Japan Society. He was a patron of the San Francisco Symphony Orchestra and an Honorable Member of the San Francisco Institute of Art. The untimely death of his beloved cousin, Anne Bremer, had fostered his interest in living artists. He never married (*Who's Who in America 1934–1935* [Chicago: A. N. Marquis, 1934] and *The Development of Modern Art in Northern California*, Part II, ed. by Joseph Armstrong Baird, Jr. [Sacramento: Crocker Art Museum, 1981], pp. 41–44).

43. Weston 1973, vol. 2, June 19, 1930, p. 168.

44. Ibid., April 2, 1927, p. 12.

45. Ibid., May 20, 1927, p. 24.

46. Ibid., March 20, 1927, p. 12.

47. Albert Bender to CK, July 26, 1927, sent c/o Thomas Cook & Son, Paris, Bender Papers.

48. Arrival date indicated by Kanaga's passport, WPE.

49. Interview with Wallace Putnam by SML, September 16, 1988.

50. CK, Concarneau, to Albert Bender, July 7, 1927, Bender Papers.

51. This feeling of disappointment with men was reinforced when she met a charming married couple with "advanced ideas." She wrote, "The man decided I imagine quite suddenly that he cared for me and gave me to understand alone and before his wife that he was quite prepared to part from her at any moment." She recalled that just a few years earlier she had gone through the same experience with "Donald" (Litchfield) ("Practically overnight and for no reason he looked upon me as a stranger . . . almost an enemy . . . and we had shared so much together") and added: "Tho I believe in leaving a mate if it is not a fine and inspiring partnership yet in this case . . . the woman is superior in many ways, in spite of a charm he has" (CK, Concarneau, to Albert Bender, July 7, 1927, Bender Papers). For her remarks about art colonies, see CK, Concarneau, to Albert Bender, undated [probably July 1927] (letter begins: "Your long letter from your bed . . ."), Bender Papers.

52. CK to Albert Bender, August 28, 1927, Bender Papers.

53. CK, Concarneau, to Albert Bender, July 22, 1927, Bender Papers.

54. CK, Concarneau, to Albert Bender, undated [probably July 1927] (letter begins: "Your long letter from your bed..."), Bender Papers.

55. CK, Concarneau, to Albert Bender, undated [probably August 1927] (letter begins: "Am having a little rest here in bed . . . "), Bender Papers.

56. Ibid.

57. CK, Paris, to Albert Bender, undated [probably late August 1927] (letter begins: "This letter has been hovering. . ."), Bender Papers.

58. CK, Paris, to Albert Bender, undated (letter begins: "Just a little note to say good morning."), Bender Papers.

59. CK, Vienna, to Albert Bender, October 28, 1927, Bender Papers. Kanaga refers to Rivera as the "Diego Baby" in a number of letters.

60. CK, Vienna, to Albert Bender, [November] 3 (incorrectly dated September 3), 1927, Bender Papers. When Kanaga returned home, however, she experimented with photo collage, among other techniques (see fig. 39).

61. Ibid.

62. CK, Nuremberg, to Albert Bender, October 15, 1927, Bender Papers.

63. CK, Vienna, to Albert Bender, October 27, 1927, Bender Papers.

64. CK, Vienna, to Albert Bender, undated (letter begins: "Oh what a day."), Bender Papers. The Wiener Werkstätte, a group that defined (through arts and crafts) the post–Art Nouveau style in Europe, grew out of the William Morris workshop and C. R. Ashbee's Guild of Handicraft in England. The school lasted from 1903 to 1932. When Kanaga visited it, the address was Döplergasse 4 in Vienna. The founders were Josef Hoffmann and Koloman Moser, designers. See Werner J. Schweiger, *Design in Vienna, Weiner Werkstätte* (New York: Abbeville Press, 1984).

65. CK, Florence, to Albert Bender, December 1, 1927, Bender Papers.

66. CK, Florence, to Albert Bender, December 4, 1927, Bender Papers.

67. CK, Rome, to Albert Bender, December 26, 1927, Bender Papers.

68. Ibid.

69. CK, Florence, to Albert Bender, December 4, 1927, Bender Papers.

70. CK, Rome, to Albert Bender, December 26, 1927, Bender Papers.

71. Ibid.

72. CK, Kairouan, to Albert Bender, January 25, 1927, Bender Papers.

73. Ibid.

74. Barry McCarthy, Kairouan, to Albert Bender, March 21, 1928, Bender Papers.

75. Postal telegraph cable from CK to Albert Bender, April 12, 1928: "Statement correct please cable balance Cooks, Paris. Consuela" (handwritten across cable: "Cabled by Thomas Cook & Son 484.10. All cables paid for by me for this and previous remittances. A.M.B."), Bender Papers.

76. CK, 9 Charles Street, New York, to Albert Bender, May 19, 1928, Bender Papers.

77. CK, New York, to Albert Bender, undated [late spring 1928] (letter begins: "Thanks for the postal card . . . "), Bender Papers.

78. CK, New York, to Albert Bender, undated [summer 1929] (letter begins: "So many envelopes and bundles . . . "), Bender Papers.

79. CK, 9 Charles Street, New York, to Albert Bender, May 19, 1928, Bender Papers.

80. CK, New York, to Albert Bender, undated [summer 1929] (letter begins: "So many envelopes and bundles . . . "), Bender Papers.

81. CK, New York, to Albert Bender, September 12, 1928, Bender Papers.

82. CK, New York, to Albert Bender, November 17, 1928, Bender Papers.

83. CK, New York, to Albert Bender, undated [Thanksgiving Day, 1929] (letter begins: "Have just developed 50 negatives . . . "), Bender Papers. She continues: "I would be very, very much pleased to see a proof of the portrait Edward [Weston] made of you . . . but I haven't the one I did of you [fig. 15], which was quite good, I think." Kanaga here seems anxious that Bender might prefer Weston's portrait to her own.

84. He left on an unspecified errand. CK, New York, to Albert Bender, undated [Christmas Day, 1928] (letter begins: "I wanted to send you a little greeting . . . "), Bender Papers.

85. Ibid.

86. CK, New York, to Albert Bender, undated [spring 1930] (letter begins: "Started a long letter to you yesterday . . . "), Bender Papers.

87. CK to Albert Bender, undated [possibly summer 1930] (letter begins: "The children have lessons in an old barn and their gardens . . ."), Bender Papers.

88. CK, New York, to Albert Bender, undated [spring 1930] (letter begins: "Started a long letter to you yesterday . . . "), Bender Papers.

89. CK, San Francisco, to Edward Weston, January 2, 1931, Edward Weston Archives, Center for Creative Photography, University of Arizona, Tucson.

90. Ibid.

91. Weston 1973, vol. 2, December 10, 1931, p. 234.

92. See Tucker 1978, pp. 3, 4.

93. One of her photographs in the show, depicting the hands of the pianist Henri Deering in performance, appeared in *The San Francisco Chronicle* (June 12, 1932. Photograph by Consuelo Kanaga, caption: "Consuelo Kanaga, San Francisco artist photographer contributed this study of the hands of Henri Deering, pianist to the 'Showing of Hands' at the M. H. de Young Memorial Museum"). Another photograph made about the same time (plate 1) was probably the second print included in the exhibition.

94. Tucker 1978. For information concerning the formation of f.64 and the first exhibition, see Deanna Kastler, *Group f.64* (San Francisco: Fine Arts Museums of San Francisco, M. H. de Young Golden Gate Park Memorial Museum, 1978); Allen Porter, "Group f.64," *Camera* 5, no. 2 (February 1973): 3; letter (of rebuttal) from Willard Van Dyke, March 8, 1973, "Group f.64" file, Photography Department, The Museum of Modern Art, New York; John Humphrey, "The Henry Swift Collection of The San Francisco Museum of Art," *Camera* 5, no. 2 (February 1973): 12 (this article also rebutted by Willard Van Dyke, in George Craven, "Group f.64 and Its Relations to Straight Photography in America," master's thesis, Ohio University, 1958).

95. Taped conversation between CK and Lawrence Saphire about Group f.64, October 23, 1977, archives of Jean S. Tucker, Center for Metropolitan Studies, Saint Louis, University of Missouri.

96. Ibid.

97. Ibid. Kanaga noted that the reviewer referred to two "pin sharp" portraits of Frances.

98. Ibid.

99. Ibid.

100. See *The San Francisco Chronicle,* November 17, 1932, "Police Insult Charged by S.F. Women"; November 18, 1932, "Police Map Own Law in Browbeating"; November 19, 1932, "Police Apology Given Women Over Insult"; November 20, 1932, "Negro League Plans Protest"; November 22, 1932, "Police Destroy Prints of Negro Chauffeur."

101. Information on McDaniel is scarce and contradictory. McDaniel wrote a short story about his first encounter with Kanaga and an art critic, Junius Cravens (Eluard Luchell McDaniel, "The Model," unpublished manuscript from Adeline Kent's Notebooks, courtesy Richard Lorenz).

102. After fighting in the Spanish Civil War with the Lincoln Battalion, McDaniel was wounded and returned to the States, remaining active in the labor movement until he was declared subversive in 1950. He died an embittered man in 1985, but he never forgot Kanaga. He visited her when he could and continued to depend upon her for occasional assistance as late as 1954. See "Radical Elders Oral History Project," interview by Peter N. Carroll and Bruce Kaiper, unpublished manuscript, 1978, courtesy of Peter N. Carroll. McDaniel refers to Junius Cravens as Julius Kraybourne in this interview; the interviewers may have had difficulty in understanding him clearly, since he was having trouble with his speech at the time, according to Peter Carroll. See also Peter N. Carroll, *Keeping Time: Memory, Nostalgia, and the Art of History,* part 3, chapter 16, "Historical Inventions" (Athens, Ga.: University of Georgia Press, 1990), and Eluard Luchell McDaniel to CK, March 13, 25, 1954, WPE.

103. Telephone interview with Chick Brown by BHM, October 14, 1991.

104. Interview with Lester Balog and Sam Brody, by Anne Tucker, September 23, 1974, transcript courtesy of Anne Tucker, Department of Photography, The Museum of Fine Arts, Houston.

105. See William Z. Foster, *Pages from a Worker's Life* (New York: International Publishers, 1939); William F. Dunne, *The Great San Francisco General Strike* (pamphlet) (New York: Workers Library, 1934); Mike Quin, *The Big Strike* (Olema, Calif.: Olema Publishing Company, 1947).

106. Interview with Lester Balog and Sam Brody by Anne Tucker, August 23, 1974, transcript courtesy of Anne Tucker, Department of Photography, The Museum of Fine Arts, Houston. Date of "smuggled into Western Worker Newspaper" was July 17, 1934.

107. Kanaga 1937, pp. 22, 23.

108. Telephone interview with Chick Brown by BHM, October 14, 1991.

109. Telephone interviews with Amos Kanaga, Jr., by BHM, June 25, 1991; with Chick Brown by BHM, October 14, 1991. Interview with Chick Brown by SML, March 31, 1990.

110. According to Walter Rosenblum, the former Secretary of the Photo League.

111. Interview by letter with CK by Anne Tucker, response received between May 26 and June 29, 1975, courtesy of Anne Tucker, Department of Photography, The Museum of Fine Arts, Houston.

112. Interview with Jack Manning by BHM, April 27, 1991.

113. Interview with Aaron Siskind by BHM and SML, June 15, 1990.

114. Ibid.

115. Interview with Jack Manning by BHM, April 27, 1991.

116. Interview by letter with CK by Anne Tucker, response received between May 26 and June 29, 1975, courtesy of Anne Tucker, Department of Photography, The Museum of Fine Arts, Houston.

117. Max Yavno, lecture at University of Houston, November 28, 1978.

118. Ben Maddow, *The Photography of Max Yavno* (Berkeley: University of California Press, 1981), n.p.

119. Interview with Jack Manning by BHM, April 27, 1991.

120. CK, New York, to Albert Bender, undated (answered: March 2, 1936), Bender Papers.

121. "Written in Blood, Mrs. Merriweather's Story," *Labor Defender* 11, no. 11 (November 1935): 4.

122. Edward Steichen, quoted in *The Christian Science Monitor,* August 16, 1948.

123. Alice (Lewisohn) Crowley, Switzerland, to CK, July 7 (no year), WPE.

124. CK, New York, to Albert Bender, undated (answered: March 2, 1936), Bender Papers.

125. Interview with Wallace Putnam by SML, September 16, 1988.

126. Frankel 1978.

127. CK, New York, to Albert Bender, undated [c. 1936] (letter begins: "Upon returning from Maine . . . "), Bender Papers.

128. Wallace Putnam to Marjorie Content and Jean Toomer, June 1, 1957, Marjorie Content Papers, courtesy of Susan Sandberg: "It was showing you Manhattan Manners that met me my present wife."

129. Interview with Susan Sandberg, daughter of Marjorie Content and Harold Loeb, by BHM, June 11, 1991; interviews with Sally Avery by BHM and SML, January 23, 1990; with Zelda Benjamin by BHM and SML, May 21, 1991.

130. Personal communication to BHM from Kristina Amadeus.

131. Sidebar by Wallace Putnam in Bates 1978.

132. Wallace Putnam to Jean Toomer, May 8, 1936, Marjorie Content Papers, courtesy of Susan Sandberg.

133. Toomer not only was a disciple of Gurdjieff, but also taught at the Gurdjieff institute in Fontainebleau, just outside of Paris, in 1924. Toomer took Gurdjieff's message to Harlem in 1925 and Chicago from 1926 until 1933. It was a philosophy based on salvation through selfless labor. Despite his influence on the Harlem Renaissance, Toomer did not identify with those writers, preferring to think of himself "as a new kind of man, a blending of races, an American." He was, he said, "of the human race" (*The Wayward and the Seeking: A Collection of Writings by Jean Toomer*, ed. and with an intro. by Darwin Turner [Washington, D.C.: Howard University Press, 1980], introduction).

134. Interview with Sally Avery by BHM and SML, January 23, 1990.

135. Telephone interview with Lee Bennett Schreiber by BHM, July 13, 1991. Kanaga photographed Schreiber's children and used them as models for her *Woman's Day* assignments. According to Schreiber, Kanaga ran screaming in frustration into Baptist Church Road every few months.

136. Interview with Wallace Putnam by SML, November 11, 1988; telephone interview with Lee Bennett Schreiber by BHM, July 13, 1991.

137. Wallace Putnam to Marjorie Content, December 13, 1941, Marjorie Content Papers, courtesy of Susan Sandberg.

138. Berenice Abbott, *A Guide to Better Photography* (New York: Crown Publishers, 1944), "Fight!" plate 27.

139. Interview with Wallace Putnam by SML, November 11, 1988.

140. Wallace Putnam, quoted in Frankel 1978.

141. Wallace Putnam to CK, undated [c. May 1937], WPE.

142. Wallace Putnam to CK, undated [c. 1945], WPE.

143. Interview with Wallace Putnam by SML, September 16, 1988.

144. Wallace Putnam to CK (two letters), undated [c. late 1940s], WPE.

145. *In and Out of Focus: A Survey of Today's Photography*, April 6–July 11, 1948. *Photographic Pioneers*, May 21–July 5, 1948. *50 Photographs by 50 Photographers: Landmarks in Photographic History*, July 27–September 26, 1948.

146. CK, New York, to Albert Bender, New York, undated (answered: March 2, 1936) (letter begins: "To prove that you are often in my thoughts . . .").

147. Interview with Wallace Putnam by SML, September 16, 1988.

148. *The Sun* merged with the *New York World Telegram* in 1950, forming the *New York World Telegram and Sun*.

149. Mitchell 1979, p. 158. She continued: "I usually ate out or had a little something to eat in the darkroom. But I would forget about eating for days. I was very fond of having a clean, shiny, waxed and beautiful studio, but aside from that I'm no housekeeper."

150. Interview with Rose Treat by BHM and SML, June 6, 1990.

151. Interview with Winn Smith by BHM and SML, February 3, 1990.

152. Interview with Sally Avery by BHM and SML, January 23, 1990.

153. Bates 1976.

154. Telephone interview with Florence Lewisohn by BHM, October 11, 1991. Kanaga had introduced Florence to Walter Lewisohn, a neighbor on Baptist Church Road, and after they married, the two couples became fast friends.

155. Telegram, CK to Edward Steichen, August 2, 1953, The Museum of Modern Art, New York, Consuelo Kanaga Artist File, indicates that Kanaga was back in New Mexico.

156. CK to Marjorie Content Toomer, undated [c. 1969, the year of Alexander Bing's death, which is mentioned in letter] (letter begins: "Yesterday came your letter and the package . . ."), Marjorie Content Papers, courtesy of Susan Sandberg.

157. Kanaga's desire to photograph Native Americans is expressed in a letter to Florence Lewisohn (letter addresses her as "Davy") in an undated letter sent c. 1952 (WPE): "This past year has been a turning point for Buddy [Walter Lewisohn] in his work. Now I really wish I had been along doing some stills. . . . Our night in the pueblo was wonderful. The mood of a pueblo as night fell. The visits from the Indian relatives etc."

158. Interview with Florence Lewisohn by BHM, October 11, 1991.

159. CK to Marjorie Content, undated [spring 1964] (letter begins: "When we don't hear from you for a while . . ."), Marjorie Content Papers, courtesy of Susan Sandberg.

160. Yvette Horgan, "A Peace Walk Recorded," *Patent Trader* (Mt. Kisco, N.Y), February 6, 1964. Information on the peace walk drawn from this article.

161. With some reluctance and at Putnam's urging, Kanaga wrote to Lucille and Charles Plotz, accepting their invitation. She had wanted to travel to Ireland and around Europe for a year and felt self-conscious about burdening the Plotz family and staying with them in Lacoste (personal communication from Kristina Amadeus to BHM).

162. CK to Marjorie Content, undated [soon after November 12, 1969, date of Alexander Bing's death], Marjorie Content Papers, courtesy of Susan Sandberg. Kanaga wrote, "It seems a lot of money as we have lived so close for years."

163. Nicholas Freyberg, interview by BHM and SML, June 16, 1990.

164. Interview with Helen Gee by BHM and SML, May 14, 1991.

165. Nicholas Freyberg and Peggy Freyberg, respectively, interview with Nicholas and Peggy Freyberg by BHM and SML, June 6, 1990.

166. Interview with J. Randall Plummer and Harvey S. S. Miller by BHM and SML, February 24, 1990. They said of Kanaga: "She respected and liked Berenice [Abbot] and thought she was tough. She loved the tonal quality and talked about imaging. She thought Imogen's [Cunningham] work was sentimental. She liked Stieglitz and his photography but felt that Stieglitz courted [the photographer] Carlotta Corpron." Kanaga told them, "The greatest influence on me is Steichen." The copy of *Camera Work* they purchased from Kanaga was inscribed, "To Litchfield from Al 291 January 22, 1922."

167. Letter to herself found among Kanaga's personal papers, WPE.

168. CK, quoted in Kalina 1972, p. 54.

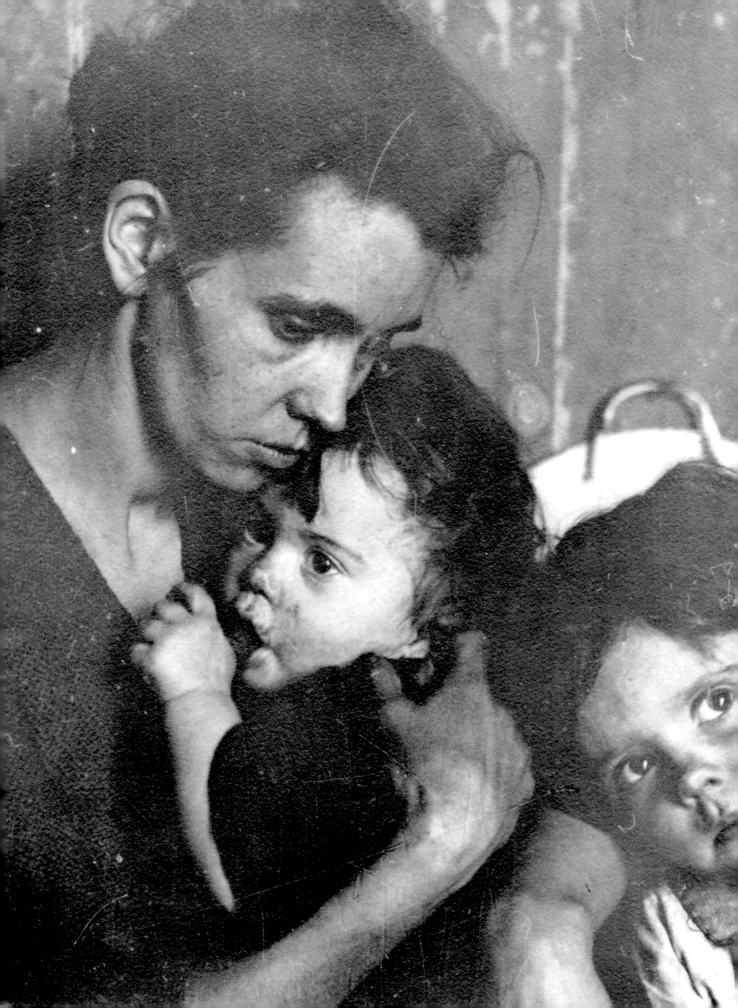

I Journalism:
Word into Image

KANAGA WAS A PIONEER female journalist photographer whose consummate professionalism led the way for the careers of Dorothea Lange and others. No matter how much she tried to depart from her early training as a newspaper photographer, she was tied to it for the rest of her life. Journalism demands quick reflex action in order to get a shot that cannot be repeated. The picture must be composed in the camera. Kanaga recalled that using the large-view camera required that "you organized your picture carefully, using the whole frame." It demanded a disciplined eye: "I remember when I started on the newspaper I learned just the fundamentals of printing and developing, no nuances. Everything had to be sharp, etched on the glass plates. When I'd do a job and come back, they'd be put on a rack— a whole row of glass plates. The editor would look up and down the row to see the sharp cut line. And, if anything wasn't so sharp he'd say, 'What's the matter, losing your eyesight?'"[1]

After hundreds of assignments, the camera becomes an extension of one's body. Instantaneously the photographer brings together focus on the subject, emotional impact, and composition of figures. One's job depended on it. Where Kanaga departed from the ordinary journalist's approach was in her choice of subject matter, in her deliberate composition, in her meticulous printing, and, finally, in her heart.

Fire (plate 5) demonstrates Kanaga's total professionalism. She has moved in as close as possible, creating a tableau of the three women. The central figure, her face contorted by grief, leans against the body of the woman behind her, who seems almost to be supporting her in her arms. The hand is deceptive: at first appearing to belong to the rear figure, it adds to the illusion of the older woman's total collapse. The face of the rear figure is solemn, but the eyes are focused on the camera. A young girl to the right of the grieving woman regards her with pity but also a kind of curiosity. From the lower right-hand corner, the eye of a spectator stares into the camera. Weegee (the press photographer Arthur Fellig) could do no better in the boldest of his photo-

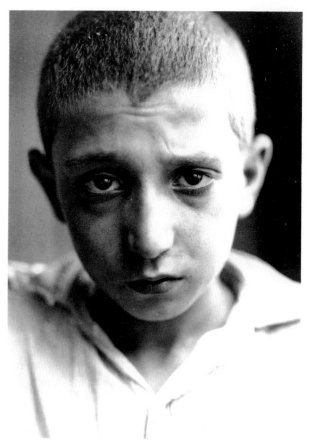

Fig. 41. *Poor Boys* (New York), 1928
Modern print from negative
82.65.1154

Fig. 42. *Malnutrition* (New York), 1928
4³/₈ x 3¹/₈
82.65.318

graphs taken in the 1940s with a four-by-five Speed Graphic using midget-size bulbs and Eastman Super Pancro Press type B film stopped down to f.16. Although Kanaga was probably using a Graflex at this time, which was adequate for outdoor photography, she routinely used flash powder for emphasis. She later explained: "We didn't have exposure meters in those days. You had to guess how the light was going to be. And we didn't have strobes for flash. We used powder. I remember Victor powder was one I used with a flash gun, and you would put what powder you needed for a certain exposure. As I look back at some of these old negatives they are just utterly beautiful, more beautiful than with a big blast of strobe because you could keep them delicate and light to fit the type of darkness, or lightness, or size."[2] In this powerful shot, for all her sensitivity to her subjects, Kanaga has invaded privacy with a shocking directness; she could push her camera into the face of a grieving woman if she had to.

In 1922 Kanaga took a job photographing for the Christmas and Relief Fund of *The New York American*, making only three or four photographs and taking several months to complete the assignment. One of these, *Mother with Children* (plate 6), is especially moving. A tired young mother holds a grubby little girl tightly in her arms. Both are dressed in dark clothing. The mother, in profile, gazes down at her daughter in despair. The child, her thumb held firmly in her smudged mouth, looks hungry. Her eyes are lifeless. Part of the face of another child in the lower right-hand corner stares directly into the camera, her expression serious. A white enamel pan, hung on the clapboard wall behind her head, forms a halo. This picture has been cropped in some versions to remove the second child, ensuring the traditional newspaper photo of contemporary madonna and child at Christmas. Kanaga printed both versions several times but mounted the shot that included only one child. Both versions are signed, indicating that Kanaga liked them equally. They are taken from a glass-plate negative, although she was using a Graflex at the time for much of her work. Flash has been used to emphasize the faces of the children, while the mother has been printed in partial shadow. The image is strong, gripping, and timeless. Another of Kanaga's images for *The New York American* shows a tubercular woman and her twelve-year-old son. The woman, ravaged by disease, looks more like the child's grandmother. Years later, Kanaga described her encounter with her subject: "I thought she was marvelous looking. I asked her if I might photograph her, and she said, 'Photograph a bony old woman like me?'" To which Kanaga replied: "Yes, I like bones."[3] The picture of the fragile, desperate woman, quite apparently starving, gazing hollow-eyed into the camera while a handsome and painfully thin young boy sits protectively by her side, is intensely affecting.

The picture titled *The Widow Watson* (plate 7) is another example of Kanaga's ability to dramatize tragedy. The photograph bears its message in an almost impersonal way, its image neither sentimental nor pitiful. It portrays the subjects with dignity and a certain haunting beauty. The mother died shortly after the picture was taken, and Kanaga tried without success to adopt the boy.[4]

A favorite picture of Kanaga's, *The Bowery* (plate 8) is very nearly an abstraction despite her involvement with social documentary photography

Fig. 40. *Poor Boy* (New York), 1928
7 1/4 x 4 7/8
82.65.171

Fig. 43. *Ray Robinson* (Albany, Georgia), 1963
13 1/4 x 10 1/4
82.65.400

and her background in journalism. A strange and powerful picture, it is a study in composition and tonality. No attempt has been made to emphasize the personal plight of the three Bowery bums. One lies curled in a wooden box that is flanked by another who crouches beside him to the right and a third who stands looking down on him. Kanaga burned (overexposed) this print in the areas around the heads and dodged (underexposed) the bodies to assure great contrast. Thus the faces are dark and unreadable, while the bodies are highly detailed; Kanaga purposely printed to depersonalize the situation. Again in *Man on Bench* (plate 9), a depiction of poverty avoids an intimate confrontation with human suffering, instead presenting an iconic synthesis of the tragedy of impoverishment. One explanation for this distance may be that Kanaga found it more and more difficult to invade the privacy of helpless people. (She felt less compunction with poor children, portraying them with obvious pathos, in *Malnutrition* [plate 10] and *Tenement, Child on Fire Escape* [plate 11], among others (figs. 40–42). The element of beauty and restraint in many of her depictions of the destitute and the oppressed is also consistent with her conviction that photography, which "could change the world," was a sacred trust.[5]

Kanaga photographed as a journalist for the last time in March 1964. Nearing seventy and already beginning to suffer from emphysema, she undertook a journey to Albany, Georgia, where she stayed for nine days and lived with a group of young peace walkers. She recorded their arrest and release as a favor to a friend, the poet Barbara Deming (fig. 35), in a series of documentary photographs. They are relatively undistinguished, workman-like shots taken by a professional news cameraman. Some of them, like *Ray Robinson* (fig. 43), relate to the work Kanaga did for radical periodicals in the thirties and forties in their idealization of the politically disenfranchised. The trip proved tiring physically and emotionally for Kanaga, who said: "I don't feel I'm young enough to stand the rigors of peace walks. But I'm heart and soul for peace and integration and if my camera can be of help I want to use it to the fullest."[6] She saw no brutality in Albany but admitted that she was scared and alienated by the unfriendly behavior of the local residents and police. Like the good news photographer she always was, Kanaga stayed her ground and recorded it all.

B.H.M.

NOTES

1 . Kalina 1972, p. 53.

2 . Bates 1976.

3 . Mitchell 1979, p. 168.

4 . Wallace Putnam, quoted in Frankel 1978.

5 . Blue Moon/Lerner-Heller Gallery 1974, p.17.

6 . Yvette Horgan, "A Peace Walk Recorded," *Patent Trader* (Mt. Kisco, N.Y.), February 6, 1964.

Plate I. *Hands*, 1930

Plate 2. *Tenements* (New York), 1939

Plate 3. *Man with Rooster* (New York), mid–late 1930s

Plate 4. *Annie Mae Merriweather, 1935*

Plate 5. *Fire* (New York), 1922

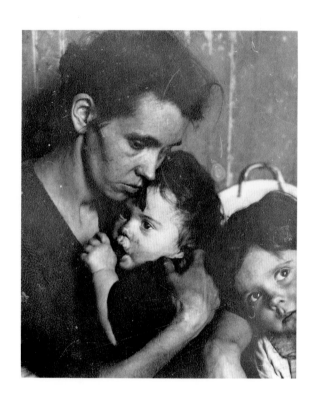

Plate 6. [*Mother with Children*] (New York), 1922–24

Plate 7. *The Widow Watson* (New York), 1922–24

Plate 8. *The Bowery* (New York), 1935

Plate 9. [*Man on Bench*] (New York), 1920s

Plate 10. *Malnutrition* (New York), 1928

Plate 11. [*Tenement, Child on Fire Escape*] (New York), mid–late 1930s

II North African Journey

AFTER TEN YEARS of earning her living as a working photographer in San Francisco and in New York, Kanaga was eager for a firsthand look at European photographic practice. During her trip abroad in 1927, in addition to viewing monuments and churches, she conscientiously sought out all opportunities to see photography: in museums, in galleries, and in artists' studios. Kanaga kept a journal of her impressions—new techniques, new possibilities of expression—until she was "overflowing with ideas and different problems . . . to work out."[1] With each passing week, she became more and more impatient for a darkroom.

It had been Kanaga's intention upon leaving California in the spring of 1927 to travel for several months on the Continent and then set up a studio, either in New York or in a European capital. Although she had not planned to go to Africa, she spent a productive four months photographing in Kairouan, Tunisia, from January until April 1928. Kanaga was stimulated by the small expatriate community of artists and writers as well as by the extraordinary light of North Africa that had captivated such artists as Delacroix, Klee, and Matisse. While her mind adjusted to the living conditions of the people of Tunisia—the widespread poverty, illness, and filth—her eye began to dwell on new formal possibilities. She wrote to Bender:

> Kairouan is one of the three holy cities of Africa. It is really . . . primitive and lovely. . . . There is much poverty and suffering here . . . poor beggars, old, lame, blind, diseased, and women carrying babies on their backs, pinched children with old faces. . . . But the little city is a delight with swaying pepper trees and continual movement of white caped figures. . . . I feel the desire to express something . . . to make a series of photographs. . . . The most interesting part of the city here is the cloud effect against the creamy white towers of the city. Such delicate tone values. I long to try and get the effect in photography.[2]

The richest sources of Kanaga's photographs of North Africa are three small albums [3] in which she presents a composite view of Kairouan—prototypes for projects she hoped to publish on San Francisco and on the

Sierras. (Several years later she began two similar projects—one, a group of photographs of African Americans, and the other, a portfolio of images of New York City.[4]) It is apparent from these exquisite compilations that three subjects preoccupied Kanaga during her North African sojourn. First, she resumed her interest in how people live—their work and daily activities. Indeed, the streets of Kairouan offered her myriad subjects. Fellow photographer Louise Dahl kept a diary, an eloquent and detailed description of life in Kairouan. Of the main street, Dahl wrote: "Kairouan at mid-day—on the Rue Saussier vibrates with the life playing busily over its surface. Street vendors, with trays balanced artfully upon their heads —call in a sing song melody, the merits to be found in their wares. Back and forth the heavily laden burros—weighted down with great mounds of fresh green grass—ply their trade of supplying fodder to the camels in the fondouks, and winding in and out [of] the heavily congested street, pass the silent seated Arabs nestled contentedly against the walls, unmindful of the swarms of flies."[5] Several photographs (plates 12–14) are representative of the sights Kanaga saw daily, images that go beyond mere description but stop short of becoming picturesque. Her intuitive compassion distinguishes these photographs, which are grounded in material reality and also convey the extraordinary harshness of life as well as the overwhelming beauty of the region.

Second, Kanaga's North African work bears the mark of her attention to formal qualities of photography—light, pattern, composition—evident in her European images. The simplicity and economical composition of several images may be seen in relation to her recent awareness and appreciation of the "primitive Italian painters" and Egyptian and the Archaic Greek sculpture she had seen in Italy.[6] Although Kanaga takes as her starting point life in Kairouan, she concentrates on geometric patterns and composition (plates 15–17). One of her most spare images, *Telephone Pole Against the Sky* (plate 18), is a pointed comment on the incongruity of the austere, indigenous architecture, dating back centuries, with the modernized innovation of electricity. *Women on a Street, Kairouan* (plate 19) demonstrates Kanaga's discerning eye: it is a tour de force of counterpoint—the white headdress against the dark wall and the trio of women silhouetted against the dazzling white building—while still revealing the flavor of daily life in Kairouan. Her witty, portraitlike image of two camels (plate 20) is striking for its lack of superfluous detail: she presents only the bobbing heads of these ubiquitous beasts, indifferent to the photographer.

Finally, throughout her stay in Kairouan, Kanaga was fascinated by the people of North Africa. Her photographs of men, women, and children (plates 21–25) reveal them as people first, never as anthropological subjects. Unlike most European and American travelers who photographed in Africa, Kanaga presents the Tunisians as individuals, with individual traits, mannerisms, and personalities, in large part because her photographs record her personal interactions.[7] During her four-month stay, Kanaga gained an insight and understanding into a way of life and a people, and thus, the photographs she produced impart a sense of Kairouan. This was the standard she applied in future projects: more than a record of a city, her photographs form a document of an experience.

S.M.L.

NOTES

1. CK, Paris, to Albert Bender, August 1927; CK, Nuremberg, to Albert Bender, October 15, 1927, Bender Papers. Special thanks to Martin Antonetti, Librarian in Special Collections, Mills College.

2. CK, Kairouan, to Albert Bender, January 25, 1928, Bender Papers.

3. One album is housed with the Bender Papers at Mills College Library, Special Collections, and two are in the Louise Dahl-Wolfe Papers, Center for Creative Photography, University of Arizona, Tucson.

4. Images of blacks are a prominent feature of Kanaga's work. Wherever she was—San Francisco, Paris, New York—she was keenly aware of the conditions of people of African descent and hoped to produce a portfolio of images that would be the basis of a book. See *U.S. Camera 1942*, p. 70, as well as her letter from New York to Bender, c. February 15, 1936, Bender Papers.

5. Louise Dahl-Wolfe Papers, Center for Creative Photography, University of Arizona, Tucson.

6. Kanaga expresses her admiration and interest in the frescoes and sculpture she saw in Italy in a number of letters to Bender, Bender Papers.

7. The May 1929 issue of *Asia* published a pictorial essay entitled "Dwellers in Holy Kairouan," with eight photographs by Kanaga, all portraits, with the exception of an image of a baby's feet (plate 15).

Plate 12. [*Sheep Herder*] (North Africa), unretouched, 1928

Plate 13. [*Man on Donkey*] (North Africa), 1928

Plate 14. [*Two Donkeys*] (North Africa), 1928

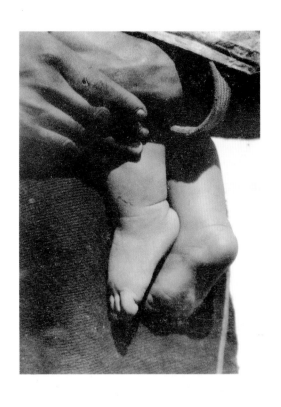

Plate 15. [*Baby's Feet*] (North Africa), 1928

Plate 16. [*Man on Horizon*] (North Africa), 1928

Plate 17. [*Horizon with Domes*] (North Africa), 1928

Plate 18. [*Telephone Pole Against the Sky*] (North Africa), 1928

Plate 19. [*Women on a Street, Kairouan*] (North Africa), 1928

Plate 20. [*Two Camels*] (North Africa), 1928

Plate 21. [*Two Children*] (North Africa), 1928

Plate 22. *[Two Children]* (North Africa), 1928

Plate 23. [*Young African*] (North Africa), 1928

Plate 24. [*Arab*] (North Africa), 1928

Plate 25. *Bedouin Girl* (North Africa), 1928

III Portraiture

Kanaga was a master at portraiture. Perhaps her greatest gift was her ability to wait . . . to wait for the unguarded moment. Sometimes, spontaneity and moving fast are everything in photography. In portraiture, it is more often the ability to stay absolutely still, to watch carefully, to talk to your subject until the camera is forgotten. The subject listens to your voice, mesmerized by your presence, sometimes relaxed enough to break eye contact. And then, as swiftly as a mongoose leaps for the head of a snake, the finger flicks.

A friend who often watched Kanaga work observed that she approached her subjects as an animal would and saw them, too, as animals: "When she photographed, she started from a distance. She would move up on them, approaching slowly. Her voice would get slower and softer. She liked to get that camera really close. By the time she finished speaking, the light fell on their skin and clothes. She had drawn them into her world."[1]

Aided by her gifts as a storyteller, Kanaga was particularly successful with children, whom she liked to photograph away from their parents (fig. 44). March Avery, daughter of Milton and Sally Avery, was one of Kanaga's favorite models (fig. 45). She remembers: "Connie talked a lot. I would do anything she asked. If she said, 'Roll down a hill,' I rolled down a hill."[2] All of Kanaga's portraits of children are solemn. She preferred to come in as close to the face as possible, just as she did with most of her subjects, despite the fact that the general rules of photography discourage moving in too close for a head shot. In one such portrait, *Young Girl in Profile* (plate 29), most of the real work was done in the printing, at which time the face was slightly overexposed, or burned, in an otherwise perfect negative. The effect is nearly that of a silhouette. The girl's face and hair are very dark, almost black; the hair ribbon, which was underexposed, or dodged, becomes luminous; the shell of the ear picks up the light accenting the dark, velvety face, as does the full and shining lower lip. The crisp white blouse makes a startling contrast. Since the negative is fairly thin and Kanaga discarded more detailed prints from that negative in perfect color balance, we know that this photograph was created in the darkroom.

Kanaga's portraits of blacks reflect her interest in the sculptural quality of their features—an interest that perhaps was stimulated by the books on African masks that she saw in Europe in 1927. In *Portrait of a Negress* (later titled *Frances with a Flower,* plate 30), the focus is so sharp that the slightly rough texture of the skin, shiny with perspiration at the hairline, seems palpable. The forehead, nose, and cheeks, highlighted by flash and dodged in the developing, contrast with the deep-set eyes lost in shadow, thus producing a sculptural dimension that turns the photograph into hills and valleys of darkness and light. The stark white blossoms pressed to the woman's nose serve only to emphasize the sensual face. This image is a hymn to the beauty of black skin and flesh that is confrontational and powerful. In *Eluard Luchell McDaniel* (plate 31), the horizontally inclined head, the four fingers masking the chin, the glittering eyes, and the splayed nose and full lips have a sculptural tactility. It is probable that this photograph—along with two of Frances (plate 30, fig. 16)—was among Kanaga's four portraits in the first f.64 exhibition of 1932.

If Kanaga's early years as a press photographer impressed upon her the value of speed and gave her the boldness to move in on her subject, her style was greatly influenced by what she saw in *Camera Work.* Her portrait of Zelda Benjamin, a young actress (plate 32), is an example of her artistic debt to Alfred Stieglitz, as is *Erica Lohman* (plate 33). Certainly Stieglitz's tonality touched her deeply. In form she was influenced by Edward Steichen, as can be seen in her portraits of the sculptors Sargent Johnson (fig. 46) and Wharton Esherick (plate 34). Her series of the folksinger Kenneth Spencer (plate 35) and *Portrait of a Man* (plate 36) are similar in mood and lighting (below the face) to Steichen's *Eugene O'Neill* and *Alexander de Salzman.* Steichen's use of dramatic lighting and contrasty printing attracted Kanaga. She also admired his deceptively simple and confrontational arrangement of the head and hands. Her romantic and dramatic *Wallace in His Studio* (plate 37) is pure

Steichen. Even Kanaga's late photograph *W. Eugene Smith and Aileen* (fig. 47) is related to Steichen's *"Mr. and Mrs."* (of the Carl Sandburgs), 1925, in composition and lighting.

Her commercial photography was also affected by Steichen's commercial work in the twenties and thirties, which was direct, pure, and well lit with seemingly simple composition. Nevertheless, she quickly learned to use her early journalistic experiences to her own advantage and developed a quality all her own in her compelling portraits of lesser-known artists and unknown friends, such as her profiles of Harvey Zook (plate 38) and Kenneth Spencer (plate 39) and her marvelous full-length portrait of Morris Kantor (plate 40).

Kanaga's creativity was best exemplified by her perfectionism in the darkroom. She constantly experimented with formulas (fig. 48). Steichen generously gave her several of his formulas for developers, which she kept and used for the rest of her life. Several other photographers gave her recipes, but she preferred Steichen's mixture of potassium bromide, Elon, soda sulphite (anhydrous), pyrosallic acid (pyro), and sodium carbonate. To this she would sometimes add metal salts. She used several variations of this mixture, some of them lethal. She dried and flattened her prints under sheets of ¼-inch plate glass, leaving them for several days. Besides toning her prints, especially the portraits, she then went over the edges of the figure with negroe pencil, a soft graphite that brings out the highlights and adds luminosity (often mistaken in her prints for degeneration or silvering). She would then smudge the lines with her fingers. On close examination, the pencil becomes evident, as in *Portrait of a Woman (M.C.)* (plate 41), and *Eiko Yamazawa* (plate 42). She used only pencil to spot her prints.

Kanaga's cropping of her portraits, in particular, showed her boldness and imagination. She cropped in the ground glass, on the negative, in the enlarger, and finally on the print itself (see plate 26). In order to bring the face

Fig. 50. *Countee Cullen*, c. 1930s
10 × 8
82.65.366

of her subject into the face of the viewer, she never hesitated to trim the picture radically at top and bottom. She composed the figure so that the hands were frequently touching or near the face, and then she often eliminated everything except the hands and face, even chopping off the top of the hairline to bring the forehead into prominence. She had no qualms about removing an extra child if the composition of mother and one child proved stronger. This gave her imagery a tight, compact energy.

These experiments in cropping were mostly used in her personal work and in her photographs of her artist and writer friends. She acquired such compositional tricks while working for newspapers, where the aggressiveness and emotional impact of the image were essential. They are first apparent in her portrait of *Harry Shokler* (plate 43). Her finest image of Mark Rothko, shown in a wide-brimmed hat (fig. 49), is centered on his tragic, impatient face, focusing on the radiant energy in his eyes. Her photographs of Milton Avery succeed when she uses confrontational head shots (plate 44) and fall apart in three-quarter poses. It is as though she decided that the head and the hands most intimately convey emotion while the body objectifies, distancing the viewer and the subject (see fig. 50).

Perhaps *Frances (with Daisies)* (plate 45), which Kanaga printed three different ways, best summarizes her mastery of cropping, composition, and printing. The tonal values are so dissimilar that the mood of the picture changes radically with each printing.

Kanaga brought the same technique she used in portraiture to her nudes. Moving in close and cropping dramatically, she created a spontaneous, confrontational intimacy in her female nude of 1928 (plate 46). A fascinating portrait of the head and shoulders of a young woman, apparently nude, with bobbed hair and enigmatic smile (plate 47), is strikingly provocative yet simple.

B.H.M.

NOTES

1 . Interview with Winn Smith by BHM and SML, February 3, 1990.
2 . Interview with March Avery by BHM and SML, February 20, 1990.

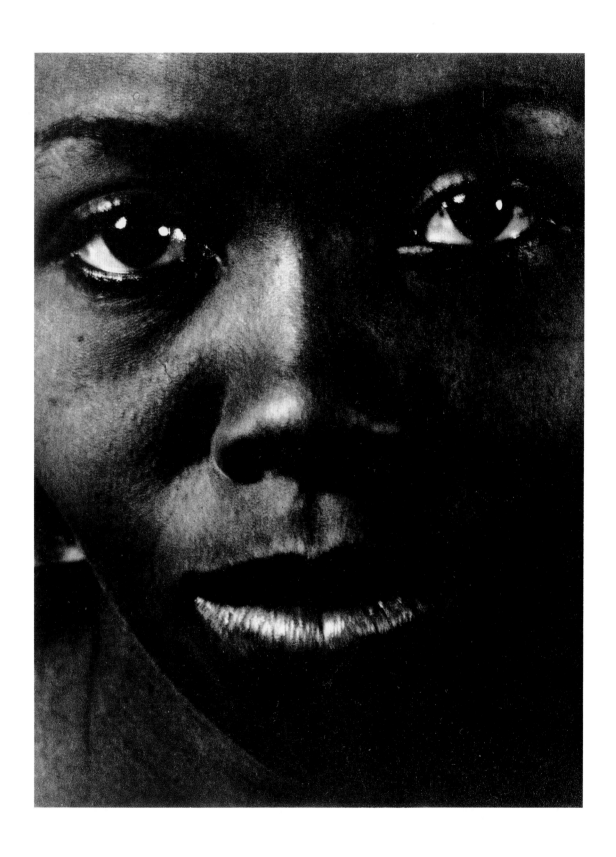

Plate 26. *Annie Mae Merriweather*, 1935/36

Plate 27. [*Native American Child*] (New Mexico), 1950s

Plate 28. *School Girl* (St. Croix), 1963

Plate 29. [*Young Girl in Profile*] (from Tennessee series), 1948

Plate 30. *Frances with a Flower*, c. early 1930s

Plate 31. *Eluard Luchell McDaniel*, 1931

Plate 32. *Zelda Benjamin*, 1941.

Plate 33. *Erica Lohman*, c. 1920s

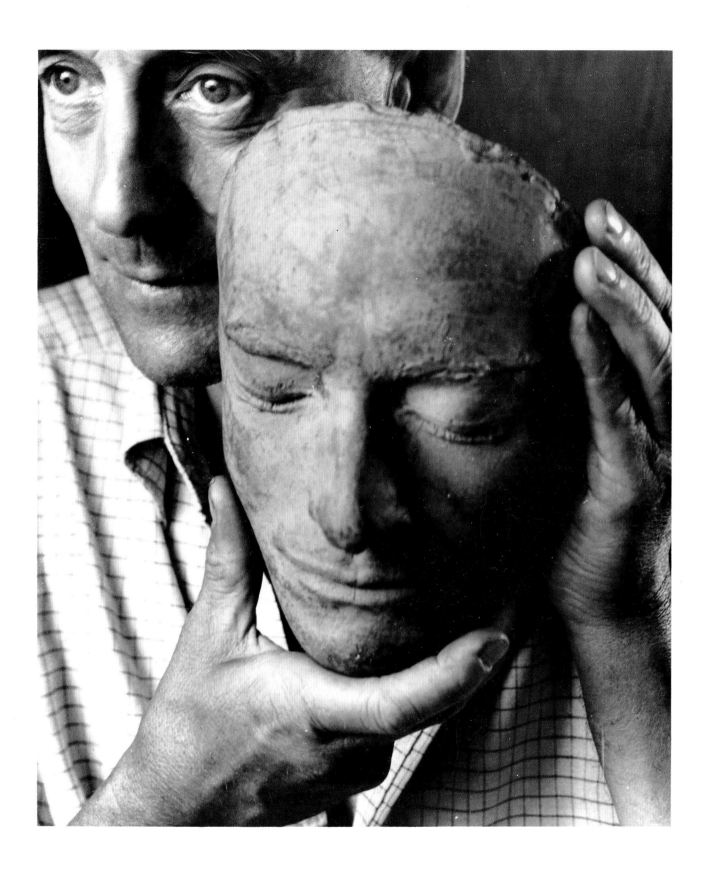

Plate 34. *Wharton Esherick*, 1940

Plate 35. *Kenneth Spencer*, 1933

Plate 36. *Portrait of a Man*, c. 1930s

Plate 37. *Wallace in His Studio*, mid–late 1930s

Plate 38. *Harvey Zook*, c. 1940

Plate 39. *Kenneth Spencer,* 1933

Plate 40. *Morris Kantor*, 1938

Plate 41. *Portrait of a Woman (M.C.)*

Plate 42. *Eiko Yamazawa*, mid–late 1920s

Plate 43. *Harry Shokler*, late 1920s–early 1930s

Plate 44. *Milton Avery*, 1950

Plate 45. *Frances (with Daisies)* (New York), 1936

Plate 46. *Nude*, 1928

Plate 47. *Portrait of a Woman*, c. 1930s

Plate 48. *Eluard Luchell McDaniel*, 1931

Plate 49. *Langston Hughes*, c. 1930s

Plate 50. *Langston Hughes*, c. 1930s

IV Images of the City

CONSUELO KANAGA's first profession was journalism, and her first subject was the city. By 1916 she was working for *The San Francisco Chronicle*, covering all aspects of city life—from a longshoremen's strike to society events. As a writer, and later as a staff photographer, Kanaga was undaunted by the places she was sent by her editor—areas where a single woman without her disregard for convention might have felt compromised.[1] She was a fearless reporter, and when, after a few years in the business, she traded her pencil for a camera, she produced sharply focused news photographs for her demanding editor—distinct and precise images that would reproduce clearly.[2] The exacting nature of her early training fostered a strict discipline that stayed with her throughout her career. Kanaga prided herself on the rigor and attention she gave the ground glass— her careful composition before snapping a photograph—and the patient care she took in the darkroom to produce a satisfactory print.

It was not until she joined the California Camera Club of San Francisco about 1918, however, that Kanaga recognized the potential of photography as an art form. Since its founding in 1890, the Camera Club had provided a place where men and, significantly, women could find instruction on photography, meet other photographers, and use the communal darkroom: in addition, it offered a forum for photographers to display their work and to give and receive informal criticism.[3] It was in the Camera Club's library—an extensive collection of books, magazines, and writings on photography[4]—that Kanaga educated herself. She must have seen Charles H. Caffin's *Photography as a Fine Art*, an essential guide since it appeared in 1900 that outlined the principles governing pictorial photography. Indeed, the soft-focused, romanticized mood of Kanaga's *Chinatown* (plate 51) displays the elements of a pictorial aesthetic, in marked contrast to what was required of her newspaper photos. It is also distinct from the well-known views of the inhabitants of Chinatown by Arnold Genthe that Kanaga admired.[5] Where Genthe was interested in documenting life in the quarter, Kanaga's superbly composed image is a mosaic of nuances of light and dark.

The volumes of Alfred Stieglitz's *Camera Work* that she encountered at the California Camera Club were a revelation to Kanaga. As she was confronted with the photographs by Edward Steichen, Paul Strand, Julia Margaret Cameron, Clarence White, Gertrude Käsebier, and Stieglitz, her concept of photography was transformed, and more important, her perceptions of herself and of her calling as a photographer were irreversibly altered.[6] Having resolved to become an artist, she determined to make a sharp distinction between her art and her commercial work, to spend less time earning a living as a news photographer, and more time experimenting with her newfound metier.

The immutable lesson of *Camera Work* was the magic use of light, and Kanaga aspired not only to discover techniques to convey in light and tone something of what lies under the surface of the image, but to meet Stieglitz, which she did shortly after her arrival in New York in January 1923. It is evident in her earliest views of New York that she chose neither Jacob Riis's nor Lewis Hine's documentary mode as her model, but instead emulated Stieglitz's style. Kanaga turned her camera to capture the awesome tumult and exhilaration of the modern working city—not its underside, but its grand bustle of activity. In an extraordinary series of images produced in 1923 and 1924, Kanaga pays homage to Stieglitz, and yet her photographs are distinguished from his by the inclusion of elements that act as anchors to the period. With the exception of *New York El* (plate 52)—a dazzling abstraction—Kanaga's tribute to modernity is never an idealized future or a timeless past, but an image organized around elements that present a material reflection of contemporary life. Scenes of East River commerce—docks, tugboats, horse-drawn wagons—are accompanied by the ever-present Brooklyn Bridge (plates 53–56), which resonates as a symbol of New York and as a monument to progress, a feat of engineering often called the Eighth Wonder of the World.[7] Its gothic arches recall the cathedrals of Europe, and Kanaga's *Downtown, New York* (plate 57) makes the allusion quite clear: the

visual resemblance between the Woolworth Building, towering over East Broadway, and Chartres Cathedral, dominating the French countryside, is unmistakable.

Although light and tonal nuance continued to absorb Kanaga, upon her return to San Francisco in 1925, she began a series of photographs of the city that are striking for their documental value as well as for their formal refinement.[8] Some of her views of San Francisco allude to nineteenth-century photographs that charted the growth of the "upstart cities" of the frontier, thereby helping to establish their legitimacy.[9] San Francisco, in particular, was a center of photographic activity, and Kanaga, like her precursors, described and therefore helped to define the evolving activities of the city. Yet in contrast to the photographs in the urban grand style of the mid-1870s—images of idealized American cities[10]—Kanaga's work focused on the life of various quarters of the city. When she took her camera to photograph Russian emigrants, she produced not simply documentary photographs, but a journalistic account of her experience, of the encounter itself. The most formal of these photographs (fig. 52) is not an objective record, but an intimate portrait of three young women. Kanaga's most successful portraits always bespeak her personal interaction and engagement with her subjects. In this case, it is apparent from the faces of the women that she has gained their confidence, in contrast to the photographs showing the more awkward pose of one of the older women (fig. 53).

It is characteristic of Kanaga's aesthetic that she never completely dislocates the subject from its specific site. For example, along Fisherman's Wharf, she fixes on the abstract quality of the fishermen's nets and the shapes of their boats (figs. 54, 55), yet she grounds the image with particulars, including the company's name, thus specifying the individual trade. Or in *Anchors* (plate 58), the formal elements of the image are counterbalanced by their depiction as tools, not simply as visually interesting industrial objects. Moreover, Kanaga depicts many facets of San Francisco life, relying on late

afternoon light and prominent shadows to capture a permeating sense of isolation and alienation in *Old Ship Hotel, Battery Street* (fig. 56).

Kanaga's experimental work was supplemented by a prosperous portraiture business with a well-to-do clientele. She was part of a dynamic community of San Francisco artists—painters, dancers, photographers, and sculptors, many of whom she photographed (figs. 9, 10). Her friends included painters Ray and Peggy Boynton; sculptors Beniamino Benevenuto Bufano and Sargent Johnson (fig. 46); dancers Margaret Nichols and Ruth St. Denis; writers Kathryn Hulme (fig. 57) and Ella Winters; photographers Annie Brigman, Louise Dahl (fig. 11), Dorothea Lange, and, when they were in town, Tina Modotti and Edward Weston. Many of them, including Kanaga, received financial support from art patron Albert Bender (fig. 15). It was Bender who encouraged her to make the "grand tour" of Europe, and Kanaga was impatient for a chance to see photographic practices abroad for herself, especially anticipating great discoveries in Munich, Berlin, and Vienna.[11] Moreover, she had saved a considerable sum with which to buy photographic equipment and hoped to return with a camera, several lenses, and an enlarger.

Few photographs from Kanaga's eight-month European trip survive: while those that remain do not form a cohesive whole, they do show the impact of current practices in Europe and the emergence of a modernist aesthetic in Kanaga's work. Among her views of Venice, a city that failed to win her affection (she was appalled at the continual and shameless attempts to fleece tourists) are several impressive photographs, striking for their transformation of recognizable monuments through an emphasis on abstraction. In three images (plates 59–61), patterns of shadows are played off against icons of Venice, creating visual analogies between the permanence of the architecture and the transitory qualities of light. The shadows of the pedestrians echo the clusters of columns on the façade of San Marco, just as the broken cloud formation mimics the lacy decorations that crown the Duomo.

Kanaga's European excursion seems to have afforded her only the briefest glimpse into the way ordinary people lived; neither did she become distracted by national events.[12] Thus, Kanaga was able to concentrate on formal problems and experiment with techniques she had observed abroad, continuing to construct images that demonstrate her sense of discovery. Her European photographs emphasize composition and balance, and a preoccupation with qualities of light (plates 62–64), in lieu of any social content. It was not until she landed in North Africa that she found a cohesive subject to photograph.

S.M.L.

NOTES

1. Riess 1968, pp. 87–88.

2. Kalina 1972, p. 53.

3. Palmquist 1989, pp. 288–89.

4. For a discussion of the impact of the California Camera Club on photographic practice in the early twentieth century, see Marjorie Mann's valuable essay in Mann 1977, pp. 7–30.

5. Dahl-Wolfe Scrapbook 1984, p. 6.

6. Kanaga specifically cites these photographers as the ones whose work she recalls having seen in *Camera Work* in her short autobiographical account in Kenega Genealogy, p. 281.

7. Tsujimoto 1982, p. 27.

8. These images have not yet been discovered as prints, but only as negatives. A collection of about forty is owned by Culver Pictures, New York.

9. Peter B. Hales, *Silver Cities: The Photography of American Urbanization, 1839–1915* (Philadelphia: Temple University Press, 1984), pp. 20–39. Hales cites Daniel Boorstin as coining the term "upstart cities."

10. Ibid., p. 284.

11. Detailed information about Kanaga's trip to Europe may be found in the Bender Papers.

12. For example, Kanaga never writes about the signs of the discord that ushered in Mussolini's rise to power that were evident throughout her stay in Italy. See Dahl-Wolfe Scrapbook 1984, p. 7.

Plate 51. [*Chinatown*] (San Francisco), late 1910s–early 1920s

Plate 52. *New York El*, 1924

Plate 53. [*Pier 27*] (from Downtown New York series), 1922–24

Plate 54. [*Horse-Drawn Wagon*] (from Downtown New York series), 1922–24

Plate 55. [*Tug and Barge, East River*] (from Downtown New York series), 1922–24

Plate 56. [*West Street with Truck*], (from Downtown New York series), 1922–24

Plate 57. *Downtown, New York*, 1924

Plate 58. [*Anchors*] (San Francisco)

Plate 59. [*San Marco*] (Venice), 1927

Plate 60. [*Piazza San Marco*] (Venice), 1927

Plate 61. [*Gondolas*] (Venice), 1927

138

Plate 62. [*Stairs*] (Perugia), 1927

Plate 63. [*Winding Road in Park*], 1927

Plate 64. [*Towers, Germany*], 1927

V An American Iconography

I F THERE IS A SINGLE DOMINANT THEME evident throughout Kanaga's work, it is her abiding interest in, and engagement with, the American scene. Many of her photographs of America resonate with the notion of a "usable past," a concept formulated by literary critic Van Wyck Brooks in 1918, which called for a revaluation of American traditions and a reconstruction of America's heritage.[1] It was not the past, however, that preoccupied Kanaga; it was the American present. And significantly, the American scene that interested Kanaga embraced people and places outside the mainstream: farm workers and cowboys, blacks and Native Americans.

The impetus for Kanaga's endeavor can be seen within a collective historical context, as well as from the specificity of her own personal history. Kanaga was subject to the cultural forces of the 1930s. She photographed for the WPA's Index of American Design—a massive accumulation of images of folk, decorative, and applied art in America from the colonial period to the Gilded Age—and thus participated in a national rediscovery (which Brooks's observations had initiated) that was at the heart of the programs of the New Deal era.[2] Yet unlike other photographers who inventoried or interpreted the multifaceted United States—its urban centers and rural areas alike—as part of the Federal Art Project, Kanaga was not circumscribed by the policies of the Farm Security Administration.[3] Her photographs are exceptional for their refusal to editorialize, and they present a viewpoint uncommonly tolerant and unprejudiced. Her compassion for the poor, for farmers, and for the working class sprang, perhaps, from her own background as a descendant of pioneers and farmers, including an active abolitionist whose home had been a station in the Underground Railroad.[4]

By disposition Kanaga resisted and disdained convention, a stance that is evident in her objective as a photographer. Unhampered by traditional notions of suitable photographic subjects or categories, Kanaga formulated her own genres that spoke to the issues that concerned her. Often, her images of Americans are not quite portraits, yet neither are they anonymous docu-

mentary images. Photographs such as *After Years of Hard Work* (plate 65) or *Mr. and Mrs. Stanley, the Adirondacks* (plate 66), among others (plates 67–72), bear the mark of her "grave honesty, reverence for the human condition, and deep respect for the ways in which people make their way in life."[5] In these images of the disenfranchised, Kanaga creates emblems of an American way of life, yet she avoids any trace of sentimentality, nostalgia, or the vulgar nationalism that accompanied much Regionalism.

When Kanaga focuses on her domestic surroundings, her images hover between genre pictures and formal studies. Photographs of a corner of her kitchen (plates 73, 74) or out her window (plate 75, fig. 58) simply record facts that exist without an artist's deliberate intervention. They form a personal history of an American photographer—a kind of "indigenous" account or record of one aspect of American culture—that Kanaga approaches both self-consciously and instinctively.

Kanaga often conveyed her emotional connection with the artifacts she photographed. Indeed, her presentation of an "American vernacular" was neither as intellectual nor as cynical as that of Walker Evans, but speaks to a specifically American experience or sense of place, a theme she had explored prior to her European tour (plate 76), and one that became more pronounced in her later work. In her correspondence with Albert Bender during her trip, Kanaga articulated a newfound appreciation for being an American citizen: "One learns when abroad how young and free ones country is and how nice in spirit. Granting that . . . many other defects . . . exist [in America] yet one feels how terrible it would be to be pressed upon on every side by foreign powers each full of old hatreds and jealousies as these European powers are."[6] Kanaga's awareness of her own American-ness was strengthened through her travels abroad, and the expatriate experience kindled a reaction that ultimately led her to discover her subject matter in an American grain.

Kanaga's treatment of landscape diverges sharply from established photographic nineteenth-century models. She drew upon neither the heroic

AN AMERICAN ICONOGRAPHY

views of nature by Carleton Watkins and others that paralleled the paintings of the Hudson River School—romantic images of the wilderness intended to champion the notion of manifest destiny—nor the pictorialist mode that domesticated nature until it became transformed into a kind of still life. Instead of memorializing scenic wonders or formulating impressionistic tableaux, Kanaga celebrated humble locales, places where traces of a human presence are visible and exist in the realm of nature. The mood of melancholy in *Clapboard Schoolhouse* (plate 77), *Child's Grave Marker* (plate 78), *Ghost Town* (plate 79), and *Barbed Wire Fence* (plate 80) issues from Kanaga's evocation of the eternal but futile human struggle against the forces of time. It is as if by seeking out facets of the American way of life that had been overlooked by other photographers, Kanaga fulfilled a moral obligation to depict an aspect of an authentic America as she saw it.

Kanaga's approach to the "American scene" was neither dogmatic nor fixed, but stemmed from her search for a truth—not simply a documentary truth, but a spiritual truth. Her photographs record uncharted territories and create an American iconography that expands and enriches our national consciousness.

S.M.L.

N OTES

1 . "On Creating a Usable Past," *The Dial* 64 (April 11, 1918): 337–41. The essay is reprinted in *Van Wyck Brooks: The Early Years: A Selection from His Works, 1908–1921*, ed. with an introduction and notes by Claire Sprague (New York: Harper & Row, Harper Torchbooks, 1968), pp. 219-26.

2 . See Alfred Haworth Jones, "The Search for a Usable American Past in the New Deal Era," *American Quarterly* 23, no. 5 (December 1971): 711–24.

3 . See Wendy Kozol, "Madonnas of the Fields: Photography, Gender, and 1930s Farm Relief," *Genders* 2, no. 2 (1988): 1–23, for an analysis of how photography was used to justify Roosevelt's agricultural policies and encourage sympathy for the victims of the Depression.

4 . Kenega Genealogy, p. 279.

5 . Kalina 1972, p. 70.

6 . CK, Florence, to Albert Bender, December 1, 1927, Bender Papers.

Plate 65. *After Years of Hard Work* (Tennessee), 1948

Plate 66. *Mr. and Mrs. Stanley, the Adirondacks (The Front Parlor)*, 1936

Plate 67. [*Native American Child*] (New Mexico), 1950s

Plate 68. [*Native American Women with Wooden Poles*] (New Mexico), 1950s

Plate 69. [*Native American Children*] (New Mexico), 1950s

Plate 70. [*Rodeo*] (New Mexico), 1950s

Plate 71. *Gus Weltie* (High Tor, New York)

Plate 72. [*Farm Family*], c. 1930s

Plate 73. *Cornelia Street Kitchen*, 1944

Plate 74. *San Francisco Kitchen,* 1930

Plate 75. [*Window Pane with View of City Yard*], c. 1930s or 1940s

Plate 76. *Seddie Anderson's Farm* (California), 1920s

Plate 77. [*Clapboard Schoolhouse*]

Plate 78. [*Child's Grave Marker*]

Plate 79. *Ghost Town* (New Mexico), 1950s

Plate 80. [*Barbed Wire Fence*] (Florida), 1950

VI Southern Portraits, Southern Labor

K ANAGA DID HER MOST FULFILLING WORK on her trips to Tennessee in 1948 and to Florida in 1950. She was happiest photographing African Americans, and the portraits she made on these trips are among her very best. *Girl with Double-Heart Ring* (plate 81) is reminiscent of her earlier *Frances with a Flower* (plate 30). While in no way idealizing the subject, this powerful portrait expresses the girl's blooming adolescence and sculptural beauty. Her hair springs with great vitality from her dark, shining forehead and pronounced features. Here is youth exploding with energy. The hand with the double-heart ring helps to frame her face. The picture is cropped to create the most potent image obtainable at a time when only images of blacks with more Caucasian features were generally admired and accepted, anticipating by forty years the wider recognition of the elegance of African features.

Kanaga had probably seen the work of Doris Ulmann, a sophisticated New Yorker who had studied with Clarence White and documented the rural population of Appalachia in the 1920s and 1930s, using a combination of social documentation and pictorialism. These idealized images of simple, patient, and noble working people, photographed with a soft-focus lens, tended to categorize blacks under the rubric of American peasant folk. The work of Dorothea Lange and other photographers of the Farm Security Administration awakened public awareness of the living conditions of destitute farmers during the Depression and drought years of the 1930s, but it was also often impersonal and sometimes lacking in spontaneity. Kanaga was determined to get as close as she could to her subjects, whom she sought to individualize. At the same time, she brought her love of composition to the project. She tried to combine an artist's eye for shape and color with a concern for human strength and dignity. Kanaga's extraordinary photograph *Mother and Son* or *The Question* (plate 82), taken with soft focus, allows the shapes of the two subjects' bodies to define the relationship between a Modiglianiesque black woman, with eyes lowered and somber expression, and a young boy who squints as he gazes up at her, as though she were the sun itself to him. *Young Girl, Tennessee* (plate 83), and *Young Girl (White Blouse), Tennessee* (plate 84),

Fig. 60. [*Three Children*], 1949/50
Gelatin silver toned print
4 x 3
82.65.238

are part of a series that also included *Young Girl in Profile* (plate 29). The photographs included in this section are less stylized and sadder than *Young Girl in Profile* and lack the innocence that gave the other photograph from the series its special beauty. In these images we can see that the subject is not the child she appears to be in *Young Girl in Profile,* but a young woman. Kanaga's *Young Mother with Baby Girl* (plate 85) is a joyous depiction of motherhood, a black madonna and child, and one of her very rare images of happiness. The mother radiates her love for her daughter. Her smile, her hair, her body language, are full of energy. The portrait is very different from, and more imaginative than, the earlier, conventional *Woman with Child* (plate 86). *Child with Apple Blossoms* (plate 87), with its wide-eyed, grave little girl, her face buried in flowers, is composed somewhat like *Frances with a Flower,* without the dramatic lighting.

A quality of ineffable sadness pervades all of Kanaga's work, becoming more noticeable from the 1940s until the end of her career; the hint of melancholy in the faces of her subjects is particularly striking in her portraits of children (fig. 60). The southern portraits, especially, have an undercurrent of despair and sometimes anger, although they are never political or editorial. One photograph, *Boy with Gun* (plate 88), of a very young black child solemnly clutching a toy pistol to his chest seems to anticipate the uneasy days ahead for the South. Taken in Tennessee or Florida, it is an oddly disturbing picture. *Norma Bruce* (plate 89), in which the subject lifts one hand to shade her eyes from the sun, is evocative of all women who have worked the land to support their families. The young woman, her face weathered and seemingly carved in stone, is splendid in her dignity.

Kanaga once said: "I work very simply, with the light against me. This means that the light is shining in front of me, rather than behind me. It allows me to soften the face of my subject, to get things one normally would not get."[1] These words might describe how she photographed her best-known work, *She Is a Tree of Life to Them* (plate 90), which appeared in Edward Steichen's *Family of Man* exhibition at The Museum of Modern Art in 1955. In a 1962 article for *The New York Times Magazine,* Steichen selected this photograph as one of seven from The Museum of Modern Art's collection of five thousand prints that he considered "great from among many great works" and proof "that photography is an art just as painting and sculpture and poetry are." Kanaga's photograph was captioned by Steichen: "How completely this picture . . . speaks for itself! This woman has been drawing her children to her, protecting them, for thousands of years against hurt and discrimination."[2] Kanaga described the work as a "picture of a Black woman with two children standing near her. Her body forms the most marvelous shape, it is big and makes a big angle. I love to photograph black people, to try to capture the strength and dignity I so often find in their faces."[3] She did capture these qualities, but it is apparent that her fascination here had more to do with tone and shape, a preoccupation that grew out of her interest in painting from the late 1920s on.

Kanaga's images of southern labor were formally composed and often prearranged. Unlike her portraits, they show little evidence of spontaneity. *Farmer and Mule* (fig. 61) presents a young man wearing a beret tipped rakishly over his forehead, posed beside his mule. It is printed to emphasize the light on his nose, with the rest of his face left in darkness. Thus he becomes

the symbol of a farmer. In *Milking Time* (plate 91), the farmer and cow become a shape against the clouded sky, two creatures in such harmony that they are one form. Kanaga does not render her subjects monumental so much as universal. They are not ennobled, but abstracted into totem. In Kanaga's *Young Woman* (plate 92), the central figure, a turbaned girl, stands in a field with her cutting knife gleaming in her hand. She is proud Ruth, "who stood in tears amid the alien corn." There are several versions of this photograph that prove Kanaga intervened in the posing of the young woman and the "muck workers" surrounding her. *Field Workers* (plate 93), from the same series, is a neutral arrangement of figures gracefully balanced against a cloud-filled sky. *Field Worker* (fig. 62) is also a formal study rather than an individual portrait. Kanaga did several versions of this image as one might do sketches for a painting. They are graceful exercises in shape and composition.

After Kanaga left Florida in 1950, she traveled on to Tennessee, where she took photographs of the sculptor William Edmondson and his work (plate 94, fig. 32). Louise Dahl-Wolfe had discovered and photographed Edmondson extensively in 1939. Kanaga surely knew of Dahl-Wolfe's interest in the black sculptor, but it is unclear what brought Kanaga to his studio. She took the last photographs of Edmondson before his death in 1951.

The photographs that Kanaga took between 1948 and 1950 were her last attempts to make a portfolio of African-American subjects. Probably nothing she did afterward gave her quite so much satisfaction. They are certainly among her finest works.

B.H.M.

Notes

1. Ames 1977.
2. Edward Steichen, "Artists Behind the Camera," *The New York Times Magazine* (April 29, 1962): 62–63.
3. Ames 1977.

Left

Fig. 61. [*Farmer and Mule*] (Florida), 1950
$9^7/_8 \times 7^5/_8$
82.65.391

Right

Fig. 62. [*Field Worker*] (from the Muck Workers series, Florida), 1950
$4^1/_4 \times 4^1/_2$
82.65.137

Plate 81. [*Girl with Double-Heart Ring*] (Tennessee), 1948

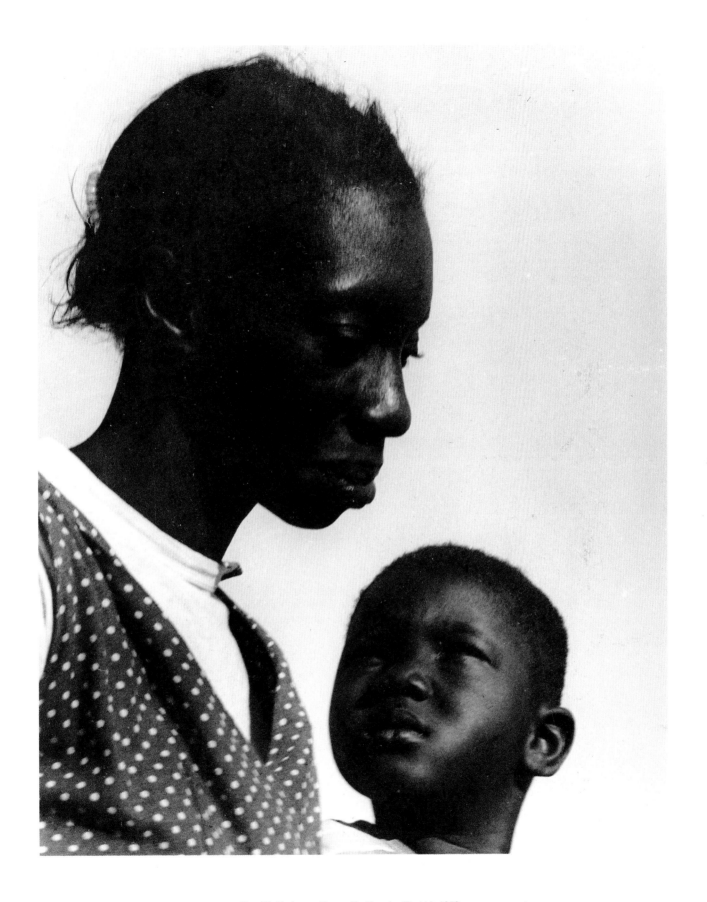

Plate 82. *Mother and Son* or *The Question* (Florida), 1950

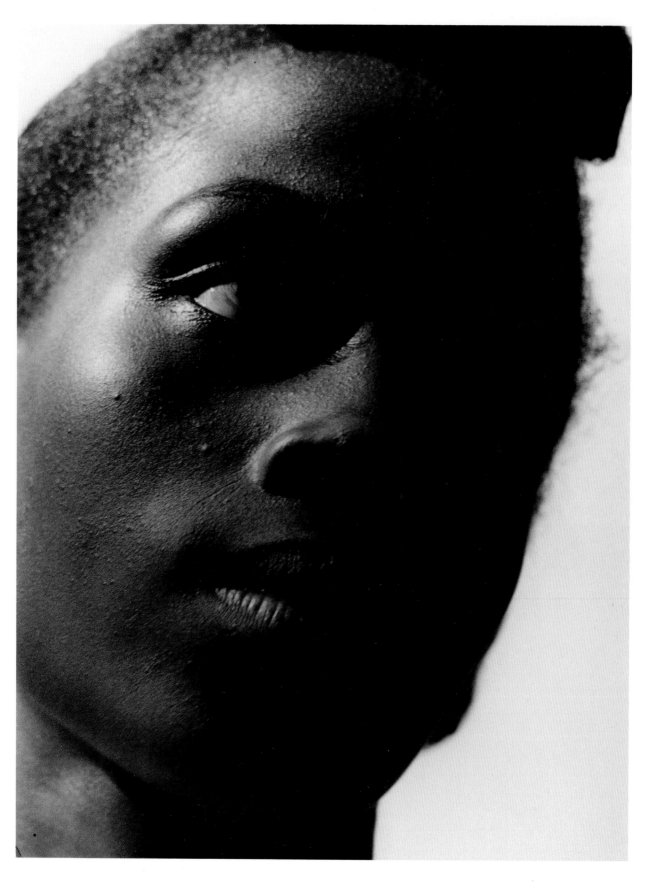

Plate 83. *Young Girl, Tennessee*, 1948

Plate 84. *Young Girl (White Blouse), Tennessee, 1948*

Plate 85. [*Young Mother with Baby Girl*] (Florida), 1950

Plate 86. [*Woman with Child*] (Tennessee), 1948/50

Plate 87. [*Child with Apple Blossoms*] (Tennessee), 1948

Plate 88. [*Boy with Gun*], 1948/50

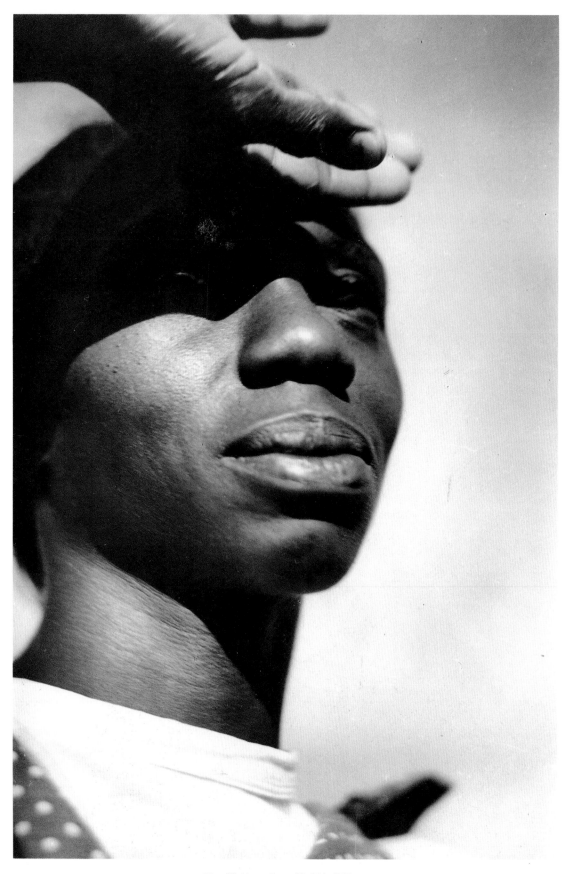

Plate 89. *Norma Bruce* (Florida), 1950

Plate 90. *She Is a Tree of Life to Them* (Florida), 1950

Plate 91. *Milking Time*, 1948

Plate 92. [*Young Woman*] (from the Muck Workers series, Florida), 1950

Plate 93. [*Field Workers*] (from the Muck Workers series, Florida), 1950

Plate 94. *William Edmondson* (Tennessee), 1950

VII Still Life Into Abstraction

AMONG KANAGA'S PHOTOGRAPHS are a number that appear to bear little resemblance to a body of work that is otherwise characterized by social veracity and a passionate portrayal of the human condition. The photographs in this group—initially emerging as still lifes and evolving into a series of studies in abstraction—may be considered in their own right, but they are not as unrelated to the rest of her photographs as a first glance might suggest. Although they form an independent motif within Kanaga's oeuvre, they echo, in a different mode, some of the considerations that inform her "social" photographs: for underlying all of Kanaga's work was her faith in a spirit or divine being and a confidence in the power of photography to evoke this spirit.

In her still lifes Kanaga first approaches the problem of how to imbue her photographs with a significance beyond the surface image. For this aspiration, Kanaga was partially indebted to Stieglitz, who maintained that through his images of objective nature, one might come to understand the artist's subjective mind—a proposition made clear in his more than 350 studies of clouds.[1] Kanaga's point of reference was less self-reflective and more universal than Stieglitz's, however, and she composed and photographed still lifes in order to suggest the possibility of an order beyond the material realm.

Kanaga's studied still lifes inevitably recall the seventeenth-century Dutch invention of the *vanitas*-type painting, which celebrated earthly delights—treasured possessions typically found in the home of a Dutch burgher—while paradoxically moralizing on the brevity and impermanence of life. While sharing the practice of meditating on objects close at hand and endowing them with transcendent significance, Kanaga breaks from the tradition by ignoring conventional symbolism and introducing her own.[2] Her approach to creating meaning bears a closer resemblance to the strategy used by William Carlos Williams, an erratic member of Stieglitz's circle. As Williams does in his most evocative poems, Kanaga strives to describe the objects with which we spend our lives, ordinary things we see and then pass

Left
Fig. 63. [*Madonna in Bell Jar*]
Modern print from negative
82.65.1984

Right
Fig. 64. [*Architectural Abstraction, New York*],
1930s or 1940s
3⅝ x 3
82.65.245

over. By paying attention to them, both photographer and poet insist on the individuality of objects, not on their similarity to other things.[3]

When she arranges and presents familiar items and domestic paraphernalia collected over the years—plants, flowers, dishes, glasses—Kanaga calls attention to their unassuming character and then invites the viewer to discover something exceptional in their very existence. The objects in photographs such as *Camellia in Water* (plate 95), *Give Us This Day* (plate 96), *Roses* (plate 97), and others (plates 98, 99; fig. 63) are invested with a deliberation that demands they be taken seriously—as if Kanaga had been making a portrait. She once commented on her photograph of a camellia that had been discarded by one of her patrons: "I thought it needed to be remembered. . . . It was so beautiful, I couldn't bear to see it so . . . unheralded."[4] Thus, the same motivation that prompted her to take pictures of America's dispossessed influenced her more abstract production.

For Kanaga, making photographs constituted a kind of religious experience, and she was unwilling to make a distinction between her own psychic development and the content of her work, writing: "I am eager to find the truth of this medium—I desire clarity in my photography and realize I must first find it in myself which is possibly more difficult."[5] She came to believe that proficiency in photographic practice would come only out of her own spiritual enlightenment. "You understand," she wrote Albert Bender, "how great a part [my work] plays in my life. And when I can balance technique on a finger point and do with it as I will—then I will probably find I have great limitations of soul and growth and have to enrichen my loam."[6]

Significantly, it was light that especially captivated Kanaga—its power to reveal meaning, its ability to define forms. She strove to wrap things in light, an idea she came to through looking at Stieglitz's photographs,[7] and, indeed, explicitly perceived photography as a process of "writing in light."[8] Kanaga often used lighting to dramatize the plain beauty and unassuming grace of the objects she photographed. The ethereal quality evident in *Flowers*

in Water (plate 100), a result of her exceptional use of light, evokes an almost spiritual aura, as if the image fulfilled an aspiration she once expressed: "If I could make one true quiet still photograph, I would much prefer it to having a lot of answers."[9]

Kanaga rarely deviated from her commitment to making content-laden photographs. In those images where she did, such as *Glasses and Reflections* (plate 101), she demonstrates her fascination with process and her mastery of the technical means necessary to perfect a print. In a more decisive break from her customary interest in content, Kanaga made a series of unapologetically abstract photographs of New York City sometime in the 1930s or 1940s (plates 102, 103; figs. 64, 65). In sharp contrast with her first images of New York, these textural studies present views of the city dislocated from the street life that had engaged her earlier. To Bender she expressed her sense of being overwhelmed by the city: "I find I can enjoy New York far more when not seeing too much of it. It is so gripping and vital and absorbing—one loses the power to feel if in daily contact with it."[10] Kanaga focused on the permanent monuments of modernity—structures such as skyscrapers and train tracks—rather than the machinery that fascinated Paul Strand or the industrial landscapes that drew Edward Weston and Charles Sheeler. The gear-and-girder technology provided Kanaga with a point of reference for her modernist aesthetic, an aesthetic that corresponded to the feeling of disaffection she felt in this "rock and granite city."[11]

In other photographs, however, Kanaga insists on a subject beyond the immediate imagery, and it is precisely her manner of introducing meaning in what might otherwise be taken as an abstract image that distinguishes her work. In *Snow on Clapboard* (plate 104), the geometric purity of the man-made architecture is mitigated by the irregularity of the snow, nature's own calligraphic mark. *Creatures on the Rooftop* (plate 105) is equally effective in balancing abstraction and transcendent meaning, as the luminosity of an evening sky passes through the "eyes" of the metal chimney tops and animates

LEFT
Fig. 65. [*Architectural Abstraction, New York*], 1930s or 1940s
3 × 4
82.65.86

RIGHT
Fig. 66. Alfred Stieglitz
Shadows on the Lake—Stieglitz and Walkowitz, 1916
4³/₈ × 3¹/₂
National Gallery of Art, Washington, D.C., Alfred Stieglitz Collection

these inanimate objects. In both images, Kanaga seems to be calling attention to the many ways a spirit—be it God, nature, or some other supreme being—makes itself visible.

For Kanaga, the process of making a photograph was as important as the final image; each photograph she took became a part of the substance of her life, even of her own mythology. At the same time, she found it hard, if not impossible, to build her life around her work: "I was much more interested in living," she said. "I think I could have done a great deal more in photography had I been less fond of daylight and day breaks."[12] Her images that synthesize these conflicts are some of her most commanding and speak to a simplicity and spirituality that Kanaga strove for her whole life. *Birches* and *Sunflower* (plates 107, 108) are breathtaking in their iconic presence: they combine meticulous composition with precise attention to light and are endowed with a clarity that averts any sentimentality. They are, in one respect, a tribute to her mentor, Stieglitz, to whom she once wrote: "It is not your technique alone but some ringing message of truth and fearlessness which has helped me in living."[13]

In the mid-1940s Kanaga began a series of dramatic photographs that took as their departure the terrain around the Icehouse, a dilapidated outbuilding situated on several acres of land in Westchester County, New York, that she and her husband purchased in 1940 and slowly turned into a home. In particular, her photographs of the surface of the pond behind her house (plates 109–12) were praised in their day for traversing new technical and interpretive photographic ground.[14] Yet despite their overt abstraction, these images do not repudiate subject matter, but contain explicit and discernible imagery: indeed, they seem to emanate a mystical quality. Kanaga finally eliminates human presence from these images. Unlike her mentor, Stieglitz, whose 1916 image *Shadows on the Lake* (fig. 66) depicts himself and a fellow artist, Kanaga puts her faith completely in a higher order. And unlike Stieglitz, whose images of clouds are bereft of any topographic clues, Kanaga grounds her photographs in nature while still achieving multiple levels of reality: the pond reflects sky, defines itself as a surface, and gives a sense of depth in an almost perfect merging of Kanaga's spiritual belief and her conviction in the transforming power of photography.

S.M.L.

NOTES

1. See Sarah Greenough, "How Stieglitz Came to Photograph Clouds," in *Perspectives on Photography: Essays in Honor of Beaumont Newhall*, ed. by Peter Walch and Thomas Barrow (Albuquerque: University of New Mexico Press, 1986), pp. 151–65.

2. See A. D. Coleman's "The Photographic Still Life: A Tradition Outgrowing Itself," *European Photography* (Göttingen, Germany) 4, no. 2 (April/May/June 1983), pp. 5–9, for insightful comments on still-life photography.

3. Charles Doyle, *William Carlos Williams and the American Poem* (New York: St. Martin's Press, 1982), p. 169.

4. Bates 1978.

5. CK, Concarneau, to Albert Bender, early August 1927, Bender Papers.

6. CK, New York, to Albert Bender, November 17, 1928, Bender Papers.

7. Interview with CK by Lawrence Saphire, October 23, 1977, Yorktown Heights, N.Y., ed. by Consuelo Kanaga, transcript courtesy of Lawrence Saphire, unpaginated.

8. Kanaga 1937, p. 22.

9. Mitchell 1979, p. 160.

10. CK, New York, to Albert Bender, [c. Christmastime, 1928], Bender Papers.

11. CK, New York, to Albert Bender, [spring 1935], Bender Papers.

12. Mitchell 1979, p. 159.

13. CK, [New York], to Alfred Stieglitz, [c. 1930–before 1946], Stieglitz Papers.

14. Kanaga's "abstract" photographs were included in numerous exhibitions during the late 1940s. See Chronology.

Plate 95. *Camellia in Water*, 1927/28

Plate 96. *Give Us This Day*

Plate 97. [*Roses*]

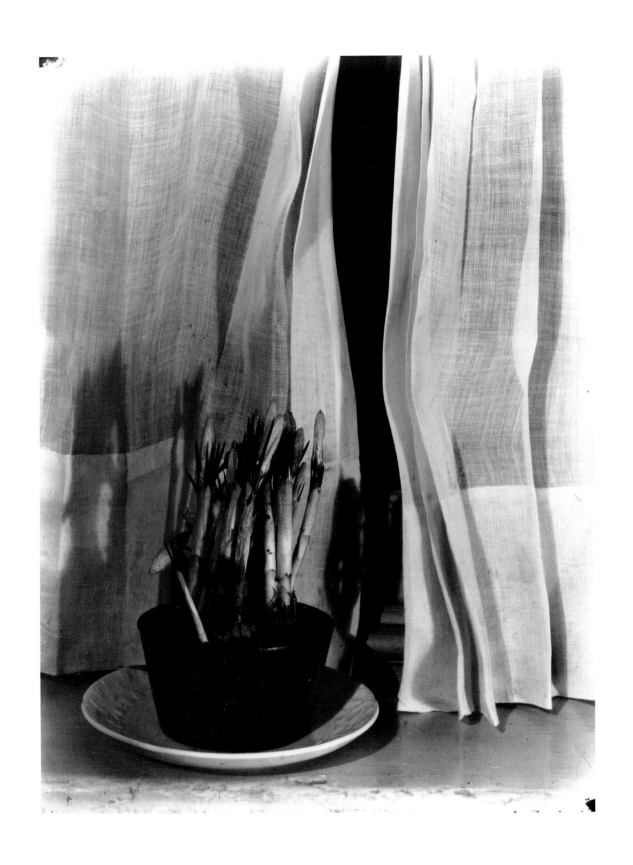

Plate 98. [*Plant and Gauze Curtain*]

Plate 99. *House Plant*, 1930

Plate 100. [*Flowers in Water*]

Plate 101. *Glasses and Reflections*, 1948

Plate 102. [*Architectural Abstraction, New York*], 1930s or 1940s

Plate 103. [*Architectural Abstraction, New York*], 1930s or 1940s

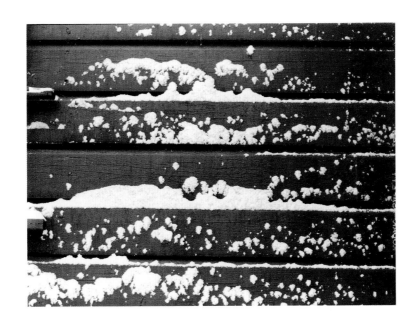

Plate 104. [*Snow on Clapboard*]

Plate 105. *Creatures on a Rooftop*, 1937

Plate 106. [*City Roofs*]

Plate 107. *Birches*, mid-1960s

Plate 108. *Sunflower*, 1942

Plate 109. *Photographing into Water*, 1948

Plate 110. [*Lily Pads*], 1948

Plate 111. *Abstraction*, 1948

112. *Abstraction*, 1948

CHRONOLOGY

1888   Mathilda (Tillie) Hartwig (1869–1953) and Amos Ream Kanaga, Sr. (1854–1927), are married.

1890   January 6: Sara Neva Kanaga, Consuelo's elder sister, born.

1894   May 25: Consuelo Delesseps Kanaga born in Astoria, Oregon; named for French diplomat and engineer Vicomte Ferdinand de Lesseps.

1895–   Amos Kanaga, Sr., a lawyer and, for a time, a district attorney in Astoria, Oregon, moves
c. 1900 his family to rural Californian towns in Monterey and Marin counties, where he pursues an interest in farming and irrigation. Eventually they settle in San Francisco, where Amos practices law and intermittently publishes small farming magazines, which his wife edits. He purchases tracts of land in Arizona and New Mexico, which he visits frequently, often taking his daughters with him.

1901   *History of Napa Valley*, compiled by Mrs. Tillie Kanaga, is published.

1906   April: San Francisco earthquake and fire.

1908   Amos Kanaga, Jr., born in San Francisco.

1911   Kanaga family living in Larkspur, Marin County.

1913   Kanaga family living on Escalle, San Francisco. Amos senior works for Western Banker.

1915   Consuelo Kanaga begins her career as a writer; works as a reporter and feature writer for *The San Francisco Chronicle*, where she stays until 1919. Kanaga family moves to 363 Page Street.

1916   Kanaga family moves to 508 Scott Street.

1916–18 Kanaga learns photographic techniques in the newspaper darkroom and by c. 1918 becomes staff photographer, covering a story on silver mines in Colorado; her first camera is an English Ensign Reflex. Joins the California Camera Club, where she discovers Alfred Stieglitz's *Camera Work;* she determines to become an art photographer. Meets many local photographers, among them Arnold Genthe, Francis Bruguière, and probably Imogen Cunningham, then Bruguière's assistant, Dorothea Lange, Edward Weston. Through Annie Brigman meets Louise Dahl (later Dahl-Wolfe), who at this time is planning to become an interior decorator but has an amateur interest in photography; they photograph the city together.

1919   At age twenty-five marries mining engineer Evans Davidson; works for the *San Francisco Daily News.*

1920   Amos senior and Tillie move to 4228 Twenty-sixth Street, where they remain; Amos works alternately as a lawyer and publisher.

1922   Kanaga departs for New York, where she hopes to meet Stieglitz; finds newspaper work in Denver and, traveling on to New Orleans, works there for a short period.

        September 18: Arrives by ship in New York Harbor.

        Shortly after arriving, finds work on *The New York American*, where her photographs are featured in "News of the Day in Pictures" and "Christmas and Relief Fund" photogravure sections; lives at 109 Bedford Street. Meets Donald Litchfield, a writer and artist who works in the Art Department at *The New York American*. By way of introduction, Litchfield sends his friend Stieglitz a print of Kanaga's photograph *Fire*.

1923   January 6: Meets Stieglitz, who shows her his photographs.

        March: Kanaga is living at 17 Christopher Street with Litchfield; attends exhibitions at Stieglitz's Intimate Gallery regularly.

        October/November: Spends a month with Litchfield in Woodstock, New York; she photographs steadily. They return to live at 182 Waverly Place.

1924   June 16: Writes Stieglitz to praise his photographs in Paul Rosenfeld's *Port of New York*.

        July 10: Kanaga and Litchfield leave for California via Chicago and Albuquerque; he remains in Capitola, near Santa Cruz, while she travels to San Francisco to begin divorce proceedings from Davidson; Litchfield lands a job in Los Angeles and moves there, while she supports herself in San Francisco, taking society portraits but leaving time for her own creative work.

        September: Kanaga goes to Los Angeles to see Litchfield; they take a trip to San Diego and Tijuana; Kanaga visits Margrethe Mather's photography studio in Los Angeles.

        December: Renews her acquaintance with Weston, who arrived back in California in late December, and remains in touch with him until he returns to Mexico in August.

Fig. 67. *Portrait of a Child*
Gelatin silver toned print
4 x 3
82.65.77

Fig. 68. *Self-Portrait in Striped Shirt*
Modern print from negative
82.65.2005

1925   February: Litchfield moves to San Francisco after he is fired by his newspaper; gets short-term jobs at newspapers doing caricatures but is generally hard up for money.

Kanaga is kept abreast of Stieglitz's enterprises through Litchfield, who receives catalogues of his shows regularly.

By July, the relationship between Litchfield and Kanaga begins to deteriorate; by the New Year, they have broken off their engagement completely.

September/October: Kanaga buys a set of *Camera Work* from Litchfield for which she pays $200.

1926   January: Advises Tina Modotti, who is visiting San Francisco from Mexico, about shopping for a new camera; mounts a small exhibition of Modotti's photographs in her studio at 1371 Post Street.

1927   By early spring has saved enough money to take the "grand tour" of Europe. Aided by Albert Bender, who acts as her accountant and probably sponsor, she leaves for Europe in March. On her way to New York, visits Weston in Glendale; picks up a number of his photographs, which he asks her to show to Stieglitz; she does so some weeks later.

June 8: Arrives in Paris at age thirty-three with a bank account of $2,000; news reaches her of her father's death on April 8; travels to the fishing village and artists' colony of Concarneau, in Brittany, where she remains until August, taking a few short excursions and painting in watercolors; reads diverse authors from Gauguin to Nietzsche to Coomaraswamy to Keyserling.

August 28: Travels to Paris to meet Louise Dahl and Anna Cohn; visits the studio of Mahonri Young, an American sculptor living in Paris.

October 2–27: Traveling alone, Kanaga visits Heidelberg, Würzburg, Rothenburg, Nuremberg (where she buys a small camera), and Munich (where she buys another lens for her Graflex).

October 27: Meets Dahl and Cohn in Vienna; buys a Zeiss lens; meets a Polish artist who teaches modern poster design at the Peoples School and who arranges for Kanaga to visit the studio of Richard Teschner.

November 15: Leaves for Budapest with Dahl; visit with Mrs. Laurvik (wife of San Francisco museum director J. Nilsen Laurvik), who acts as their guide to the city.

November 21: Kanaga and Dahl leave for Venice, where they spend about a week.

November 29–December 18: Kanaga and Dahl spend three weeks in Florence. Kanaga fashions a makeshift darkroom in their room, enabling them to develop some of their European negatives (see fig. 13).

December 18: Kanaga and Dahl travel on to Perugia, making a day trip to Assisi.

December 21–29: Spend Christmas in Rome; Kanaga and Dahl develop negatives in their quarters.

December 29: Kanaga and Dahl leave for Naples, making a side trip to Pompeii, and then travel to Palermo.

1928   January 9: Leave Palermo for Tunisia; on the ferry Kanaga meets a charismatic Irishman, James Barry McCarthy, a writer, ex-pilot, and former soccer player.

After a short stay in Tunis, Kanaga goes to Kairouan, Tunisia, where she, Dahl, McCarthy, and painter Meyer (Mike) Wolfe join writer Dahris Martin and painter Harry Shokler, both Americans, and Dutch artists R. Bonnet and Geent Huysser. Kanaga remains in Kairouan until April; she makes more than 100 negatives and plans a book on Kairouan with text by McCarthy.

March: Kanaga marries McCarthy.

Early April: Kanaga and McCarthy leave Tunisia for Paris.

By May Kanaga and McCarthy are living in New York, first at 9 Charles Street and shortly thereafter at 5 MacDougal Alley. Kanaga works for several months as a retoucher in the studio of Nickolas Muray and eventually sets up her own darkroom, alternating between portrait photography and assimilating new ideas from Europe. McCarthy ghostwrites and works on his own short stories and a play to be produced at the Provincetown Playhouse.

Summer: Eiko Yamazawa visits Kanaga in New York; a painter when Kanaga met her in San Francisco, she worked in Kanaga's studio while attending the School of Fine Arts in 1926. In New York Yamazawa works in Muray's studio as a retoucher and as Kanaga's studio assistant, then returns to Japan the next year and becomes a successful photographer.

September: Kanaga's sister, Neva Brown, visits New York, hoping to find a publisher for her children's illustrations.

Christmastime: McCarthy travels to Cannes, France, for six weeks.

1930	December: Kanaga moves with McCarthy to San Francisco into her mother's house at 4228 Twenty-sixth Street; Mathilda became a real estate agent after her husband's death.
1931	Kanaga sets up a darkroom and reestablishes her portraiture business; writes Weston in early January, inviting him to use the studio for city sittings; by 1932 she has a studio at 2506a Leavenworth Street.
	Summer: Kanaga meets nineteen-year-old African American Eluard Luchell McDaniel, an adventurer. Born on a Mississippi farm, he worked his way around the country on levee camps, and as a bootblack, waterboy, newsboy, bellhop, and automobile mechanic, coming to San Francisco in 1930; after he meets Kanaga, he works as a "houseboy" and chauffeur at her home and later, through Kanaga, finds jobs in artists' studios and as the elevator operator in an artists' studio building. Kanaga photographs McDaniel's face often. McDaniel publishes several of his short stories periodically; leaves for Spain to defend the Loyalists during the Civil War. (Kanaga kept in touch with him after she left California.)
1932	June: Kanaga's photograph of pianist Henri Deering's hands is exhibited in *Showing of Hands* at the M. H. de Young Memorial Museum, San Francisco.
	November 15–December 15: Kanaga shows with the first exhibition of Group f.64 held at the M. H. de Young Memorial Museum (members of the group were Edward Weston, Ansel Adams, Willard Van Dyke, Imogen Cunningham, Sonya Noskowiak, John Paul Edwards, Henry Swift; Kanaga, Preston Holder, Alma Lavenson, Brett Weston are invited to show). Kanaga exhibits four photographs: *Portrait of Negro I* and *II* and *Portrait of a Negress I* and *II*. In all likelihood these were two portraits of McDaniel and two portraits of her friend Frances.
	November 16: Kanaga, her sister Neva, and McDaniel are taken to the Hall of Justice and subjected to lengthy questioning and insinuations by two police officers for riding in a car driven by a "negro boy"; one officer justifies his actions by saying he intends to establish unwritten Jim Crow laws for San Francisco. The incident prompts protests by the San Francisco branch of the NAACP and the local Negro Welfare League.
1934	Kanaga moves her studio to 730 Montgomery Street, the same building in which her friend photographer Roger Sturtevant works, and near Dorothea Lange, who had taken a studio at 802 Montgomery in 1928.
	During this period Kanaga becomes concerned with the union activities of the Longshoreman's Association, as does McDaniel. When the longshoremen begin their strike on May 8, Kanaga photographs clashes between strikers and the police on the waterfront of San Francisco, and the destruction of the office of the *Western Worker*.
	According to fellow photographer and activist Lester Balog, the first and only exhibition of Photo Commontors in the gallery at Gelber-Lilienthal Bookstore is closed down by the American Legion.
1935	Spring: Returns to New York without McCarthy, moving to 15 West Ninth Street. Now in her early forties, Kanaga becomes more actively involved with the political left, in large part because of her experience during the San Francisco strike.
	October: On assignment for *New Masses*, photographs Annie Mae Merriweather, whose husband, Jim Press Merriweather, had been lynched for his support of a strike by the Share Croppers Union, Lowndes County, Alabama; Swiss psychiatrist Carl Jung acquires a print from this series.
1936	Winter–spring: Attends a course on "Fundamentals of Marxism" at the Workers School. Kanaga's photographs appear as covers for *Labor Defender* in January and for *Sunday Worker* in May.
	February: Takes radical journalist John Spivak's portrait. Begins plans for a portfolio of studies of blacks; undertakes to find a family to live with in Harlem during March and April. Works on the Index of American Design, a Works Progress Administration project, for $23.86 per week. Remeets Wallace Putnam, to whom she had been introduced several years earlier through their mutual friend, photographer Marjorie Content. Putnam (1899–1989), a painter, had been doing paste-ups in the advertising department of *The Sun* since 1925, when he and Milton Avery moved to New York from Hartford, Connecticut.
	May 28: Marries Putnam at Municipal Building. Moves in with him at 59 Morton Street.
	July: In their just-purchased 1934 Ford, Kanaga and Putnam honeymoon, first at Lake George, where they visit Alfred Stieglitz, and then drive to New Hampshire, Vermont, and Massachusetts.
	December: Kanaga's photographs are featured in first issue of *Direction* (a design by Putnam is used for the cover of the next five issues); two assemblages by Putnam included in *Fantastic Art, Dada, Surrealism*, The Museum of Modern Art, New York.

Fig. 69. *New York Skyline*, c. mid-1930s
Gelatin silver toned print
8⅝ x 5½
82.65.218

Fig. 70. Cover of *20th Century Americanism*
Estate of Wallace B. Putnam

Fig. 71. *Imogen Cunningham*
4³/₄ x 4
82.65.434

1937   Kanaga travels to California to visit her mother, who has suffered a stroke.

1938   By this time Kanaga has become involved with the New York Photo League, founded in 1936 by a group that broke with the Film and Photo League. Although she did not give formal classes, Kanaga's technique influenced the younger photographers, especially Max Yavno, who introduced her to Aaron Siskind.

February 7: Lectures at the Photo League with Siskind on documentary and feature photography.

February–May: Runs a Photo League feature group, "Neighborhoods of New York," which meets three times a month.

May: Four photographs by Kanaga of the 1937 New York May Day Parade featured in *Direction.*

Beginning in July, and continuing through the fifties, Kanaga does regular free-lance work at *Woman's Day*, primarily for writers Susan Bennett Holmes and Gladys Huntington Bevans, and sporadically for *Good Housekeeping.*

December–January 1939: Runs the Photo League "Illustrative Group," which meets at her studio once a week.

1939   February: Kanaga is a member of the Sponsoring Committee for an Exhibition of American Photography at the World's Fair.

September: Receives an honorable mention for her photographs exhibited at *How New York Lives*, sponsored by the Citizens Housing Council.

1940   Kanaga and Putnam purchase the Icehouse in Yorktown Heights, Westchester County, New York, where they spend weekends and summers until 1950, when they move there permanently; Kanaga maintains a studio at 114 East Eighteenth Street. Throughout the 1940s, Kanaga and Putnam are part of an artistic circle that includes Sally and Milton Avery, Zelda and Gershon Benjamin, the Adolph Gottliebs, the Mark Rothkos, Sasha and Hella Hamid, Alexander Archipenko; later, through Mark Rothko, they meet Katherine Kuh.

1941   Buys a new camera (a Zeiss Jewel) for her free-lance work at *Woman's Day.*

1946   Summers in Provincetown.

1947   Summers in Lubec, Maine, and Gaspé Peninsula, Quebec.

1948   Living at 24 Cornelia Street.

April 6–July 11: Included in *In and Out of Focus: A Survey of Today's Photography*, The Museum of Modern Art, New York: three abstract photos exhibited. (Exhibition travels for several years, with venues at Institute of Contemporary Arts, Washington, D.C., Museum of Modern Art, San Francisco, and Henry Gallery, University of Washington, Seattle.)

May 21–July 5: Included in *Photographic Pioneers*, Addison Gallery of American Art, Andover, Mass.: four abstract photographs exhibited.

July 27–September 26: included in *50 Photographs by 50 Photographers: Landmarks in Photographic History*, The Museum of Modern Art, New York; curator Edward Steichen exhibits *Annie Mae Merriweather*, which becomes his gift to The Museum of Modern Art.

Kanaga travels to Tennessee.

Summers in Martha's Vineyard and Vinalhaven, Maine.

1949–50   November–February: Kanaga and Putnam spend four months in Maitland, Florida, joining Milton and Sally Avery at the Research Studio, an arts colony founded in the 1930s by Jules André Smith. Kanaga finds the artists' colony less stimulating than some of the local sights, such as revival churches, baseball games, and the "mucklands," where itinerant field workers find subsistence employment and where she photographs one of her best-known works, *She Is a Tree of Life to Them.*

1950   March: Leaving Florida, Putnam and Kanaga travel to Nashville, Tennessee, where she photographs sculptor William Edmondson.

The Sun merges with the *New York World Telegram*; Putnam's job becomes redundant and is terminated; Kanaga and Putnam move permanently to the Icehouse on Baptist Church Road; despite their interesting and illustrious neighbors, many of whom are writers and artists, Kanaga finds herself virtually isolated from the New York art scene. She continues photographing the terrain around her home and maintains a commercial business, taking formal portraits steadily over the next twenty-five years.

1952   Travels to California with Putnam and photographs with Imogen Cunningham and Alma Lavenson; Putnam and Cunningham visit Ojai.

1953   May 27: Tillie Kanaga dies; Kanaga and Putnam travel to California, stopping in Taos, New Mexico, in August on their way back to New York.

1955   Two photographs are included in Edward Steichen's *Family of Man*, The Museum of Modern Art, New York.

Summers in Pomequit.

1956	Putnam teaches an evening art course at the Summit Art Center in Summit, New Jersey.
	Summer spent on Grand Manan Island, New Brunswick; on their way, Kanaga and Putnam visit Jean Toomer and Marjorie Content in Doylestown, Pennsylvania, and Alexander Bing in Provincetown, Mass. They are his guests at Hans Hoffman's annual spring party.
1957	Helen Gee, founder and director of Limelight Gallery, approaches Kanaga about showing in New York; Kanaga demurs.
	March: Kanaga and Putnam spend five weeks in Mark Rothko's apartment in New York while he takes a visiting-artist position at Tulane University.
1958	Kanaga and Putnam summer in Taos, New Mexico; become friendly with Dorothy Brett, with whom they correspond for several years. During one of their many trips to Taos, Kanaga and Putnam are accompanied by their friend Walter (Buddy) Lewisohn, who was filming there.
1959	June–August: Travel west, via the northern route through South Dakota, Wyoming, and Montana; return east through New Mexico, where they visit Dorothy Brett.
1962	January: Kanaga and Putnam spend several months at the home of Buddy and Florence Lewisohn in St. Croix, acting as "foster" parents to the Lewisohn boys.
1963	Summer in Martha's Vineyard and Millbrook, New York.
1964	January: Barbara Deming invites Kanaga to Albany, Georgia, where she has been arrested with other marchers on the Quebec-Washington-Guantánamo Walk for Peace. The walk began in Quebec on May 26, 1963, and reached Miami, Florida, on May 29, 1964, after delays while walkers were jailed in Griffin, Macon, and Albany, Georgia; Deming's account was published as *Prison Notes* in 1966. Kanaga takes some of her last documentary photographs here.
	Summer: Kanaga and Putnam travel to Lacoste, France.
1965	Winter in St. Croix.
1966	Summer in Wellfleet, Mass.
1967	Travel to Lacoste, France.
1968	January 9–30: Kanaga is included in three-person exhibition at Briarcliff College Art Gallery.
	May 16: Admitted to Northern Westchester Hospital, Mt. Kisco, for major surgery.
1969	November: Alexander Bing dies; leaves Kanaga and Putnam each $2,000. His widow, Matilda Bing, eventually gives his photographic equipment and enlarger to Kanaga.
1972	Summer in Provincetown, Massachusetts.
1973	April 22–May 20: Kanaga is included in two-person show at Village Gallery, Croton-on-Hudson.
	Summers in Martha's Vineyard.
1974	May 4–June 1: Retrospective exhibition of Kanaga's photography co-sponsored by Blue Moon Gallery and Lerner-Heller Gallery, New York.
	Autumn: Kanaga breaks her leg.
1976	January 4–28: One-person show held at Photo Graphics Workshop, New Canaan, Connecticut, organized by Thomas Hammung.
	Richard Lerner assembles a retrospective of eighty works by Kanaga that is exhibited at The Brooklyn Museum (December 15–January 20, 1977) and then travels to Jorgensen Gallery, University of Connecticut, Storrs (July 12–30, 1977).
1977	January 15–April 10: One-person exhibition held at Wave Hill Center for Environmental Studies, Bronx, New York, organized by Cornelia Cotton.
	Kanaga interviewed by Terry Katz-Nelson for Channel 11 News, New York.
1978	Included in: *Group f/64*, exhibition held at University of Missouri, Saint Louis. *Recollections: Ten Women of Photography*, by Margaretta Mitchell, published (includes interview with Kanaga).
	February 28: Kanaga dies at age eighty-three in Yorktown Heights.
1979:	September 21–November 4: Included in *Recollections: Ten Women of Photography*, exhibition held at International Center of Photography, New York.
1982	November 20–January 2 1983: Exhibition of Kanaga's paintings, drawings, and photographs, Cornelia Cotton Gallery, Croton-on-Hudson, New York.
1988	Included in *Vintage Photographs by Women of the 20's and 30's*, Edward Houk Gallery, Chicago.

Fig. 72. *Marjorie Content*
Modern print from negative
82.65.610

Fig. 73. *Clouds and Mesa*
Modern print from negative
82.65.2160

AFTERWORD

Grace M. Mayer

ONSUELO KANAGA shared my belief that every exposure—whether the image of a flower or of a face, of an animal or of a human being—is a self-portrait of its creator. She found beauty in despair, physical anguish, and deterioration—that of others and that of her own.

She was a pioneer in the interpretation of the inherent beauty of African Americans. Possibly her greatest strength was in the depiction of black mothers and their children, portrayed with tender sympathy and understanding. Childless herself, she repeatedly celebrated maternity in her images. It may be that her chef d'oeuvre is the famous *She Is a Tree of Life to Them*, included in the *Family of Man* exhibition of 1955 and signalized by Steichen in his acceptance letter of November 19, 1954. He wrote that "among the prints that have been *definitely* selected as key material in the various categories of the show is one photograph of yours." The emphasis is Steichen's, and he was never given to hyperbole. He once said that his favorite photograph in the entire exhibition was this one. After his death, in 1974, Consuelo wrote to me, "I hardly knew him but he was the best friend (to my whole self that includes my work) I've ever had."

Consuelo sometimes brightened my door at the museum when she visited Steichen. One immediately felt in the presence of greatness when looking upon the majesty of her face, handsome even in the aura of illness.

In addition to her other gifts, she excelled as a technician in her darkroom mastery. In a June 1974 letter to me she wrote, "It's heaven to make a print."

Steichen always maintained that the future of photography rested in the hands of women, because of their intuitive faculties of mind. In his time he favored such diverse talents as those of Dorothea Lange, Imogen Cunningham, Lotte Jacobi, Berenice Abbott, and Consuelo Kanaga, each in their separate orbit. Consuelo herself singled out Cunningham, for she wrote in a letter to Steichen: "She is the greatest woman I have ever known in Photography. Generous, human, and brave." These were qualities often attributed to herself by others.

SELECTED BIBLIOGRAPHY

Books, Articles, and Dissertations

Alswang and Hiken 1961. Alswang, Betty, and Amber Hiken. *The Personal House: Homes of Artists and Writers.* New York: Whitney Library of Design, 1961.

Ames 1977. Ames, Lynne. "Her Photographs Capture 'Spirit of Man.'" *Reporter Dispatch* (White Plains, N.Y.), undated clipping [1977] in archives of Department of Prints, Drawings, and Photographs, The Brooklyn Museum.

Bates 1976. Bates, Connie. "Inner Light: A Conversation with Consuelo Kanaga." *The Yorktowner,* September 29, 1976.

Bates 1978. Bates, Connie. "Consuelo Kanaga Dies." *The Yorktowner,* March 8, 1978.

Blue Moon/Lerner-Heller 1974. *Consuelo Kanaga Photographs: A Retrospective.* Exh. cat. New York: Blue Moon Gallery and Lerner-Heller Gallery, 1974.

Cunningham Trust 1978. *Imogen Cunningham: Frontiers, Photographs 1906–1976.* Essay by Richard Lorenz. Exh. cat., Berkeley, Calif.: Imogen Cunningham Trust, 1978.

Dahl-Wolfe Scrapbook 1984. *Louise Dahl-Wolfe: A Photographer's Scrapbook.* Preface by Frances McFadden. London: Quartet Books, Ltd., 1984.

Dijkstra 1969. Dijkstra, Bram. *Cubism, Stieglitz, and the Early Poetry of William Carlos Williams: The Hieroglyphics of a New Speech.* Princeton: Princeton University Press, 1969.

Ehrens 1990. Ehrens, Susan. *Alma Lavenson: Photographs.* Berkeley, Calif.: Wildwood Arts, 1990.

Frank et al. 1979. *America and Alfred Stieglitz: A Collective Portrait.* Ed. by Waldo Frank et al. New York: Literary Guild, 1934. Reprint edition: New York: Aperture, 1979.

Frankel 1978. Frankel, Bruce. "Consuelo Kanaga, Pioneering Photographer." *Reporter Dispatch* (White Plains, N.Y.), April 16, 1978, Sunday Magazine.

Kalina 1972. Kalina, Judith. "From the Icehouse: A Visit with Consuelo Kanaga." *Camera 35* 1, no. 10 (December 1972): 52–55, 68, 70.

Kanaga 1937. Kanaga, Consuela [sic]. "Writing in Light." *Direction* 1 (December 1937): 22–23.

Kenega Genealogy. Kenega, Eugene. *Descendants of Johanes Gnäge and John Kenege Sr. and Related Families.* Midland, Mich.: Privately published, 1988.

Library of Congress 1980. *A Century of Photographs 1846–1946: Selected from the Collections of the Library of Congress.* Compiled by Renata V. Shaw. Washington, D.C.: Library of Congress, 1980.

Mann 1977. *California Pictorialism.* Organized by Marjorie Mann. Exh. cat. San Francisco: San Francisco Museum of Modern Art, 1977.

Mitchell 1979. Mitchell, Margaretta K. *Recollections: Ten Women of Photography.* New York: Viking Press, Studio Books, 1979.

Orvell 1989. Orvell, Miles. *The Real Thing: Imitation and Authenticity in American Culture, 1880–1940.* Chapel Hill and London: University of North Carolina Press, 1989.

Palmquist 1989. Palmquist, Peter E. "19th Century Photographers." In *Yesterday and Tomorrow: California Women Artists,* ed. by Sylvia Moore, pp. 282–97. New York: Midmarch Arts Press, 1989.

Riess 1968. "Dorothea Lange: The Making of a Documentary Photographer." Interview conducted by Suzanne Riess in 1960–61. Regional Oral History Office, Bancroft Library, University of California, Berkeley, 1968.

Szarkowski 1981. Szarkowski, John. *American Landscapes.* Exh. cat. New York: The Museum of Modern Art, 1981.

Tichi 1987. Tichi, Cecelia. *Shifting Gears: Technology, Literature, Culture in Modernist America.* Chapel Hill and London: University of North Carolina Press, 1987.

Trachtenberg 1989. Trachtenberg, Alan. *Reading American Photographs: Images as History, Mathew Brady to Walker Evans.* New York: Hill & Wang, 1989.

Travis 1979. Travis, David. *Photography Rediscovered: American Photographs, 1900–1930.* Exh. cat. New York: Whitney Museum of American Art, 1979.

Tsujimoto 1982. Karen Tsujimoto. *Images of America: Precisionist Painting and Modern Photography.* Exh. cat., San Francisco Museum of Modern Art. Seattle and London: University of Washington Press, 1982.

Tucker 1978. *Group f.64*. Intro. by Jean Tucker. Exh. cat. Saint Louis: Center for Metropolitan Studies, University of Missouri, 1978.

Van Haaften 1989. *Berenice Abbott, Photographer: A Modern Vision*. Ed. with introductions and checklist by Julia Van Haaften. Exh. cat. New York: New York Public Library, 1989.

Vanderbilt 1980. Vanderbilt, Paul. "The Arnold Genthe Collection." In Library of Congress 1980 (see above), pp. 85–95.

Weston 1973. Weston, Edward. *The Daybooks*, vols. 1 (Mexico) and 2 (California). Ed. and introduced by Nancy Newhall. Millerton, N.Y.: Aperture, 1973.

Published Reproductions by Consuelo Kanaga

The authors are indebted to Kristina Amadeus for generously sharing the material on Kanaga in the Estate of Wallace Putnam. Many items therein are newspaper clippings for which full bibliographic information is unavailable.

1929

McCarthy, Consuelo, and Barry McCarthy. "Dwellers in Holy Kairouan." *Asia Magazine* 29 (May): 392–95. Ills.: eight untitled photographs from Kairouan.

1932

The San Francisco Chronicle, June 12. Ill.: photograph of Henri Deering, pianist, Kanaga's contribution to an exhibition at the M. H. de Young Memorial Museum, *Showing of Hands*.

Photo 1932. Paris: La Revue, Arts et Métiers Graphiques. Ill: p. 82, no title (*Eluard Luchell McDaniel*).

1934

Photo 1933–4. Paris: La Revue, Arts et Métiers Graphiques. Ills: p. 57, no title (*Kenneth Spencer*); p. 109, no title (*Frances with a Flower*).

1935

"Notes." *Story* (New York) 6, no. 31 (February): 4, 99–101. Ill.: p. 101, "Luchell." Also in this issue, "2 or 3 Stories by Luchell," pp. 30–34.

New Masses 17, no. 4. (October 22): 17. Ill.: *Annie Mae Merriweather*.

1936

Labor Defender (January). Ill.: cover.

Sunday Worker, May 3. Ill.: *Friends*, cover.

1939

U.S. Camera 1940. Ed. by T. J. Maloney. New York: Random House. Ills.: p. 145, no title (*Kenneth Spencer*); p. 146, no title.

n.d. [c. 1939–40]

20th Century Americanism. Ill.: cover.

1940

U.S. Camera 1941. Photo judge, Edward Steichen. Ed. by T. J. Maloney. New York: Duell, Sloan & Pearce (a U.S. Camera Book). Color ill: p. 34, *Michael*.

1941

U.S. Camera 1942. Photo judge, Edward Steichen. Ed. by T. J. Maloney. New York: Duell, Sloan & Pearce (a U.S. Camera Book). Ill.: p. 68, *Opus I* (*Frances*); p. 69 *Opus II* (*Eluard Luchell McDaniel*).

1942

U.S. Camera 1943. Photo judge, Lt. Camdr. Edward Steichen, USNR. Ed. by T. J. Maloney. New York: Duell, Sloan and Pearce (a U.S. Camera Book). Ill.: p. 74, *Early Morning, New York*.

1948

Review of *50 Great Photographers*. *The Christian Science Monitor*, August 16. Ill.: *Annie Mae Merriweather*.

1955

U.S. Camera 1956. Ed. by Tom Maloney. New York: U.S. Camera Publishing Corp. Ill.: p. 138, *Tree After Ice Storm*.

The Family of Man. Exh. cat. New York: The Museum of Modern Art. Ills.: p. 32, no title (*She Is a Tree of Life to Them*); p. 162, no title (*Young Girl, Tennessee*).

1958

Bachtel, Louise Seaman. "Margaret Wise Brown." *Horn Book* (June): 173–86. Ills.: portraits of Margaret Wise Brown.

Patent Trader (Mt. Kisco, N.Y.), December 18. Ill.: *Annie Mae Merriweather.*

Photography of the World: 1958. Tokyo: Heibonsha Publishers. Ill.: p. 10, *Child with Apple Blossom.*

1962

Steichen, Edward. "Artists Behind the Camera." *The New York Times Magazine*, April 29, pp. 62–63. Ill.: *She Is a Tree of Life to Them*, p. 63.

1964

Interracial Review: Journal of Christian Democracy 37, no. 1 (January). Ill.: cover, *She Is a Tree of Life to Them.*

Horgan, Yvette. "A Peace Walk Recorded." *Patent Trader* (Mt. Kisco, N.Y.), February 6. Ill.: photograph of peace marchers.

1968

Review of exhibition at Briarcliff College Art Gallery. *Citizen Register* (Ossining, N.Y.), January 6. Ill.: *Annie Mae Merriweather.*

1974

Hoffman, Marla. "Consuelo Kanaga." *World Magazine*, June 29, pp. 6–7. Ills.: *School Girl, St. Croix; The Widow Watson; The Camellia; Annie Mae Merriweather; Poor Boy; Frances with a Flower; Mark Rothko; San Francisco Kitchen.*

1978

Segal, Edith. "Two Women: Innovators and People's Artists." *Daily World*, March 8. Ill.: *The Widow Watson.*

Archival Material

Public Institutions

Archives of American Art, Smithsonian Institution, Washington, D.C. Imogen Cunningham Papers

Beinecke Rare Book and Manuscript Library, Yale University, New Haven, Connecticut. Alfred Stieglitz Collection, Yale Collection of American Literature: Stieglitz-Kanaga Correspondence; Stieglitz–Donald Litchfield Correspondence.

Center for Creative Photography, University of Arizona, Tucson. Louise Dahl-Wolfe Papers; Edward Weston Papers.

Mills College, Special Collections, Oakland, California. Albert Bender Papers.

The Museum of Modern Art, New York. Photography Department. Edward Steichen Artist File; Consuelo Kanaga Artist File.

Personal Archives

Estate of Wallace B. Putnam

Judith Kalina

Susan Sandberg

Lawrence Saphire

Margaretta Mitchell

Interviews

March Avery and Philip Cavanaugh, interview by Barbara H. Millstein and Sarah M. Lowe, February 20, 1990, New York.

Sally Avery, interview by Barbara H. Millstein and Sarah M. Lowe, New York, January 23, 1990.

Zelda Benjamin, interview by Barbara H. Millstein and Sarah M. Lowe, May 21, 1991, Berkeley Heights, New Jersey.

Chick Brown, interviews by Sarah M. Lowe, October 7, 1988, and March 31, 1990, Mill Valley, California; telephone interviews by Barbara H. Millstein, July 13, 1991, and October 14, 1991.

Cornelia Cotton, interview by Barbara H. Millstein and Sarah M. Lowe, January 8, 1990, Croton-on-Hudson, New York.

Louise Dahl-Wolfe, interview by Sarah M. Lowe, June 9, 1989, Paramus, New Jersey.

Nicholas and Peggy Freyberg, interview by Barbara H. Millstein and Sarah M. Lowe, June 16, 1990, Martha's Vineyard, Massachusetts.

Helen Gee, interview by Barbara H. Millstein and Sarah M. Lowe, May 14, 1991, New York.

Hella Hamid, interview by Sarah M. Lowe, April 24, 1990, Los Angeles.

Mrs. John R. Harrison, telephone interview by Barbara H. Millstein, May 30, 1991.

Judith Kalina, interview by Sarah M. Lowe, May 31, 1991, New York.

Amos Kanaga, Jr., interview by Sarah M. Lowe, March 31, 1990, San Mateo, California; telephone interviews by Barbara H. Millstein, March 25, 1991, and June 25, 1991.

Katherine Kuh, interview by Barbara H. Millstein and Sarah M. Lowe, February 5, 1990, New York.

Barbara Kulicke and Evelyn Jones, interview by Barbara H. Millstein, June 12, 1991, New York.

Florence Lewisohn, telephone interview by Barbara H. Millstein, October 11, 1991.

Helen Coule Lurie, telephone interview by Barbara H. Millstein, June 13, 1991.

Jack Manning, interview by Barbara H. Millstein, April 27, 1991, New York.

William Maxwell, interview by Barbara H. Millstein and Sarah M. Lowe, January 9, 1990, New York.

Helen Meredith, telephone interview by Sarah M. Lowe, May 23, 1991.

Margaretta Mitchell, interview by Sarah M. Lowe, March 1990, Oakland, California.

Susan Copen Oken, interview by Barbara H. Millstein, July 8, 1991, New York.

J. Randall Plummer and Harvey S. S. Miller, interview by Barbara H. Millstein and Sarah M. Lowe, February 25, 1990, Ambler, Pennsylvania.

Wallace Putnam, interviews by Sarah M. Lowe, September 16, 1988, and November 11, 1988, Yorktown Heights, New York.

Susan Sandberg, interview by Barbara H. Millstein, June 11, 1991, Doylestown, Pennsylvania.

Lee Bennett Schreiber, telephone interviews by Sarah M. Lowe, March 1990; by Barbara H. Millstein, July 13, 1991.

Aaron Siskind, interview by Barbara H. Millstein and Sarah M. Lowe, June 15, 1990, Pawtucket, Rhode Island.

Winn and Lawrence Beal Smith, interview by Barbara H. Millstein and Sarah M. Lowe, February 3, 1990, Cross River, New York.

Rose and Lawrence Treat, interview by Barbara H. Millstein and Sarah M. Lowe, June 16, 1990, Martha's Vineyard, Massachusetts.

LENDERS TO THE EXHIBITION

Zelda Benjamin
Center for Creative Photography, University of Arizona, Tucson
Estate of Wallace B. Putnam, Courtesy of Kristina Amadeus
International Center of Photography, New York
Mills College Library, Special Collections, Oakland, California
Museum of the City of New York
Charles and Lucille Plotz
Naomi and Walter Rosenblum
San Francisco Museum of Modern Art
Shokler Family, Courtesy of Cornelia Cotton Gallery, Croton-on-Hudson, New York

PLATES

The following list of plates (and the figures indicated at the end) represents the exhibition checklist. Exceptions are plates marked with asterisks, which are not included in the exhibition.

Plate 1. *Hands*, 1930
7$^1/_2$ x 12
82.65.2248

Plate 2. *Tenements* (New York), 1939
13$^1/_2$ x 10$^5/_8$
Museum of the City of New York, Gift of the Citizen's Housing Council of New York, Inc., 39.265.17

Plate 3. *Man with Rooster* (New York) mid–late 1930s
5$^1/_2$ x 4$^1/_4$
82.65.395

Plate 4. *Annie Mae Merriweather*, 1935
Gelatin silver toned print
13 x 10$^1/_8$
82.65.379

Plate 5. *Fire* (New York), 1922
4$^3/_4$ x 3$^3/_4$
Unretouched
82.65.23

Plate 6. [*Mother with Children*] (New York), 1922–24
3$^5/_8$ x 3
From glass plate negative
82.65.413

Plate 7. *The Widow Watson* (New York), 1922–24
3$^5/_8$ x 3
82.65.450

Plate 8. *The Bowery* (New York), 1935
Gelatin silver toned print
9$^1/_2$ x 11$^3/_4$
82.65.383

Plate 9. [*Man on Bench*] (New York), 1920s
4$^5/_8$ x 3$^5/_8$
82.65.911a

Plate 10. *Malnutrition* (New York), 1928
10$^1/_2$ x 9
82.65.447

Plate 11. [*Tenement, Child on Fire Escape*] (New York), mid–late 1930s
6$^7/_8$ x 3$^7/_8$
82.65.315

Plate 12. [*Sheep Herder*] (North Africa), 1928
4$^1/_8$ x 6$^1/_4$
Unretouched
82.65.2651

Plate 13. [*Man on Donkey*] (North Africa), 1928
Modern print from negative
82.65.2133

Plate 14. [*Two Donkeys*] (North Africa), 1928
4$^3/_8$ x 5$^1/_8$
Unretouched
Estate of Wallace B. Putnam

* **Plate 15**. [*Baby's Feet*] (North Africa), 1928
3$^{15}/_{16}$ x 2$^5/_8$
Center for Creative Photography, University of Arizona, Tucson

Plate 16. [*Man on Horizon*] (North Africa), 1928
5$^1/_8$ x 3$^5/_8$
Unretouched
82.65.81

* **Plate 17**. [*Horizon with Domes*] (North Africa),1928
2$^{13}/_{16}$ x 3$^3/_4$
Center for Creative Photography, University of Arizona, Tucson

Plate 18. [*Telephone Pole Against the Sky*] (North Africa), 1928
Modern print from negative
82.65.2141

Plate 19. [*Women on a Street, Kairouan*] (North Africa), 1928
Modern print from negative
82.65.2138

Plate 20. *[Two Camels]* (North Africa), 1928
Modern print from negative
82.65.2131

Plate 21. *[Two Children]* (North Africa), 1928
Modern print from negative
82.65.2126

Plate 22. *[Two Children]* (North Africa), 1928
Modern print from negative
82.65.2128

Plate 23. *[Young African]* (North Africa), 1928
 Modern print from negative
82.65.2137

Plate 24. *[Arab]* (North Africa), 1928
Modern print from negative
82.65.2130

* **Plate 25.** *Bedouin Girl* (North Africa), 1928
3 $^7/_8$ x 2 $^{15}/_{16}$
Center for Creative Photography, University of Arizona, Tucson

Plate 26. *Annie Mae Merriweather*, 1935/36
7 $^7/_8$ x 5 $^7/_8$
International Center of Photography, New York

Plate 27. *[Native American Child]* (New Mexico), 1950s
Gelatin silver toned print
7 $^1/_2$ x 4 $^5/_8$
82.65.369

Plate 28. *School Girl* (St. Croix), 1963
9 $^3/_8$ x 7
82.65.407

Plate 29. *[Young Girl in Profile]*
(from Tennessee series), 1948
10 $^3/_8$ x 8 $^7/_8$
82.65.11

Plate 30. *Frances with a Flower*, c. early 1930s
Gelatin silver toned print
10 $^5/_8$ x 8
82.65.10

Plate 31. *Eluard Luchell McDaniel*, 1931
Gelatin silver toned print
5 $^3/_4$ x 7 $^3/_4$
82.65.12

Plate 32. *Zelda Benjamin*, 1941
Gelatin silver toned print and graphite
12 $^3/_8$ x 9 $^3/_8$
Collection of Zelda Benjamin

Plate 33. *Erica Lohman*, c. 1920s
4 x 3
San Francisco Museum of Modern Art

Plate 34. *Wharton Esherick*, 1940
Bromide print
9 $^1/_8$ x 7 $^3/_4$
82.65.462

Plate 35. *Kenneth Spencer*, 1933
9 $^3/_8$ x 7 $^1/_8$
82.65.368

Plate 36. *Portrait of a Man*, c. 1930s
Gelatin silver toned print
4 $^1/_4$ x 3 $^1/_8$
82.65.432

Plate 37. *Wallace in His Studio,* mid–late 1930s
Gelatin silver toned print
9 $^1/_2$ x 7 $^3/_4$
Estate of Wallace B. Putnam

Plate 38. *Harvey Zook*, c. 1940
7 $^3/_4$ x 4 $^7/_8$
82.65.73

Plate 39. *Kenneth Spencer*, 1933
7 $^3/_4$ x 4 $^1/_8$
82.65.398

Plate 40. *Morris Kantor*, 1938
9 $^3/_8$ x 7 $^1/_2$
82.65.384

Plate 41. *Portrait of a Woman (M.C.)*
Gelatin silver toned print with graphite
5 $^5/_8$ x 4 $^7/_{16}$
82.65.173

Plate 42. *Eiko Yamazawa*, mid–late 1920s
Gelatin silver toned print with graphite
7 $^1/_4$ x 4 $^1/_2$
82.65.299

Plate 43. *Harry Shokler*, late 1920s–early 1930s
Gelatin silver toned print
9 $^{15}/_{16}$ x 7 $^{15}/_{16}$
Collection of Shokler Family, Courtesy Cornelia Cotton Gallery, Croton-on-Hudson, New York

Plate 44. *Milton Avery*, 1950
Gelatin silver toned print
9 $^3/_4$ x 7 $^3/_4$
82.65.127

Plate 45. *Frances (with Daisies)* (New York), 1936
Gelatin silver toned print
9 $^5/_8$ x 7 $^5/_8$
82.65.2252

Plate 46. *Nude*, 1928
8 $^1/_4$ x 6 $^1/_8$
82.65.2245

Plate 47. *Portrait of a Woman*, c. 1930s
Gelatin silver toned print
9 $^3/_4$ x 7 $^3/_4$
Collection of Naomi and Walter Rosenblum

Plate 48. *Eluard Luchell McDaniel*, 1931
9 $^1/_2$ x 7 $^1/_2$
82.65.465

Plate 49. *Langston Hughes*, c. 1930s
Modern print from negative
Negative in Estate of Wallace B. Putnam

Plate 50. *Langston Hughes*, c. 1930s
Modern print from negative
Negative in Estate of Wallace B. Putnam

Plate 51. *[Chinatown]* (San Francisco), late 1910s–early 1920s
Gelatin silver toned print
5 $^3/_4$ x 5 $^3/_8$
82.65.139

Plate 52. *New York El*, 1924
6 $^3/_4$ x 4 $^7/_8$
Center for Creative Photography, University of Arizona, Tucson

Plate 53. *[Pier 27]* (from Downtown New York series), 1922–24
Gelatin silver toned print
9 $^5/_8$ x 7 $^1/_8$
82.65.420

Plate 54. *[Horse-Drawn Wagon]* (from Downtown New York series), 1922–24
2 $^5/_8$ x 3 $^7/_8$
82.65.401

Plate 55. [*Tug and Barge, East River*] (from Downtown New York series), 1922–24
3 1/8 x 4 1/4
82.65.160

Plate 56. [*West Street with Trucks*], (from Downtown New York series), 1922–24
4 x 3
One of five images on contact sheet
82.65.143

Plate 57. *Downtown, New York*, 1924
9 5/8 x 7 5/8
International Center of Photography, New York

Plate 58. [*Anchors*] (San Francisco)
Modern print from negative
82.65.2001

Plate 59. [*San Marco*] (Venice), 1927
6 3/8 x 8 1/4
82.65.2237

Plate 60. [*Piazza San Marco*] (Venice), 1927
Modern print from negative
82.65.2146

Plate 61. [*Gondolas*] (Venice), 1927
Modern print from negative
82.65.2145

Plate 62. [*Stairs*] (Perugia), 1927
Modern print from negative
82.65.2143

Plate 63. [*Winding Road in Park*], 1927
Modern print from negative
82.65.2144

Plate 64. [*Towers, Germany*], 1927
Modern print from negative
82.65.2150

Plate 65. *After Years of Hard Work*, (Tennessee), 1948
Gelatin silver toned print
6 1/8 x 4 5/8
82.65.387

Plate 66. *Mr. and Mrs. Stanley, the Adirondacks* (*The Front Parlor*), 1936
7 1/4 x 8 5/8
82.65.406

Plate 67. [*Native American Child*] (New Mexico), 1950s
Gelatin silver toned print
4 x 3 5/8
82.65.320

Plate 68. [*Native American Women with Wooden Poles*] (New Mexico), 1950s
Gelatin silver toned print
3 3/4 x 2 7/8
82.65.253

Plate 69. [*Native American Children*] (New Mexico), 1950s
Gelatin silver toned print
5 3/8 x 6 3/8
82.65.297

Plate 70. [*Rodeo*] (New Mexico), 1950s
Gelatin silver toned print
3 7/8 x 3 3/4
82.65.31

Plate 71. *Gus Weltie* (High Tor, New York)
Gelatin silver toned print
5 1/2 x 4 1/2
82.65.433

Plate 72. [*Farm Family*], c. 1930s
Gelatin silver toned print
9 1/8 x 6 7/8
82.65.451

Plate 73. *Cornelia Street Kitchen*, 1944
4 3/4 x 3 3/4
82.65.412

Plate 74. *San Francisco Kitchen*, 1930
9 3/4 x 7 5/8
82.65.29

Plate 75. [*Window Pane with View of City Yard*], c. 1930s or 1940s
3 3/4 x 3 3/8
82.65.239

Plate 76. *Seddie Anderson's Farm* (California), 1920s
9 1/16 x 6 7/8
82.65.404

Plate 77. [*Clapboard Schoolhouse*]
4 3/8 x 3 1/4
82.65.272

Plate 78. [*Child's Grave Marker*]
4 5/8 x 3 1/2
82.65.247

Plate 79. *Ghost Town* (New Mexico), 1950s
4 1/4 x 7
82.65.145

Plate 80. [*Barbed Wire Fence*] (Florida), 1950
4 3/4 x 7 1/2
82.65.142

Plate 81. [*Girl with Double-Heart Ring*] (Tennessee), 1948
10 3/4 x 6 3/4
82.65.463

Plate 82. *Mother and Son* or *The Question* (Florida), 1950
9 3/8 x 7 5/8
82.65.13

Plate 83. *Young Girl, Tennessee*, 1948
9 5/8 x 7 3/8
82.65.2249

Plate 84. *Young Girl (White Blouse), Tennessee*, 1948
10 5/8 x 6 7/8
82.65.2232

Plate 85. [*Young Mother with Baby Girl*] (Florida), 1950
9 1/2 x 7 1/8
82.65.455

Plate 86. [*Woman with Child*] (Tennessee), 1948/50
3 7/8 x 3
82.65.452

Plate 87. [*Child with Apple Blossoms*] (Tennessee), 1948
13 x 8 5/8
82.65.378

Plate 88. [*Boy with Gun*], 1948/50
3 15/16 x 2 7/8
82.65.34

Plate 89. *Norma Bruce* (Florida), 1950
11 3/4 x 7 7/8
82.65.365

Plate 90. *She Is a Tree of Life to Them* (Florida), 1950
12 ³/₄ x 9 ⁵/₈
Collection of Charles and Lucille Plotz

Plate 91. *Milking Time*, 1948
3⁵/₈ x 4³/₄
82.65.426

Plate 92. [*Young Woman*] (from the Muck Workers series, Florida), 1950
6³/₄ x 6¹/₂
82.65.364

Plate 93. [*Field Workers*] (from the Muck Workers series, Florida), 1950
6¹⁵/₁₆ x 8¹/₄
82.65.92

Plate 94. *William Edmondson* (Tennessee), 1950
3¹/₄ x 3¹³/₁₆
82.65.2118b

Plate 95. *Camellia in Water*, 1927/28
6⁷/₈ x 5³/₁₆
82.65.437

Plate 96. *Give Us This Day*
Gelatin silver toned print
6⁵/₈ x 7
82.65.235

Plate 97. [*Roses*]
Modern print from negative
82.65.1987a

Plate 98. [*Plant and Gauze Curtain*]
Modern print from negative
82.65.1990

Plate 99. *House Plant*, 1930
Bromide print
3 x 2⁷/₈
82.65.425

Plate 100. [*Flowers in Water*]
4⁷/₁₆ x 3¹/₄
82.65.435

Plate 101. *Glasses and Reflections*, 1948
4³/₄ x 3⁵/₈
82.65.24

Plate 102. [*Architectural Abstraction, New York*], 1930s or 1940s
4 x 3¹/₈
82.65.243

Plate 103. [*Architectural Abstraction, New York*], 1930s or 1940s
3¹⁵/₁₆ x 2¹³/₁₆
82.65.244

Plate 104. [*Snow on Clapboard*]
3 x 4
82.65.56

Plate 105. *Creatures on a Rooftop*, 1937
9¹³/₁₆ x 6¹/₄
82.65.427

Plate 106. [*City Roofs*]
2¹³/₁₆ x 3⁷/₈
82.65.331

Plate 107. *Birches,* c. mid-1960s
5 x 3⁷/₈
82.65.99

Plate 108. *Sunflower*, 1942
8³/₁₆ x 7⁷/₈
82.65.377

Plate 109. *Photographing into Water*, 1948
10³/₄ x 6⁷/₈
82.65.2238

Plate 110. [*Lily Pads*], 1948
7¹/₈ x 7
82.65.105

Plate 111. *Abstraction,* 1948
Gelatin silver toned print
9¹/₄ x 7¹/₂
82.65.121

Plate 112. *Abstraction,* 1948
Gelatin silver toned print
9¹/₂ x 7¹/₄
82.65.120

The following figures are also included in the exhibition: figs. 27, 45, 47, 51–56, 64, 65.

INDEX

Pages on which figures or plates appear are in italics.